MARINER'S MEMORABILIA

A GUIDE TO BRITISH SHIPPING COMPANY CHINA OF THE 19th. & 20th. CENTURIES

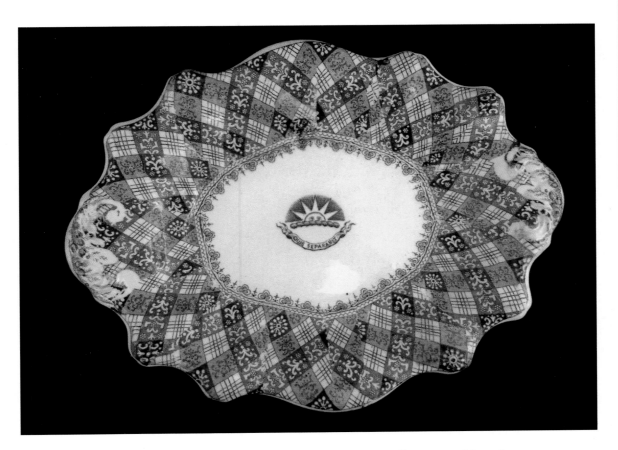

*Very early Peninsular & Oriental Steam Navigation Company china plate -
Caledonian pattern, circa 1840's*

VOLUME TWO

PLEASE NOTE

Pages 1 to 14 and Pages 311 to 323 are to be found in both Volume One and Volume Two

Pages 15 to Page 144 are to be found only in Volume One

Pages 145 to Page 310 are to be found only in Volume Two

Published by
Peter & Pam. Laister
Mariners, Gorse Way,
Hartley,
Longfield,
Kent DA3 8AE

email: mariners@anchorage65.fsnet.co.uk

Copyright © Peter Laister 2006

ISBN 0-9554058-1-5

Printed by
Wyndeham Grange
Butts Road, Southwick, West Suffolk, BN42 4EJ
(01273) 592244

PREFACE

As a small boy in North Yorkshire in the 1940's, and despite the fact there was no seafaring tradition in my family, I decided at a very early age that I wanted to go to sea as a deck officer in the Merchant Navy.

During the course of my school days I commenced collecting photographs and postcards of merchant ships, also the brochures that were issued by the shipping companies. These advertised the delights of such vessels as the "Queen Mary", "Queen Elizabeth" and "Caronia" and the beautiful liners of the Union-Castle Mail Steamship Company. My obsession with collecting, therefore, dates from the 1940's.

Having completed my education, I went to sea as a Cadet with the Ellerman's Wilson Line of Hull on their services to Scandinavia, the Mediterranean and the East Coast of the United States and Canada. After five years with the Wilson Line, I served for ten years with the Union-Castle Line as a Deck Officer, sailing on both their passenger liners to South & East Africa, and their refrigerated cargo liners. I also made several voyages on Clan Line vessels and served for nine months on the "Nina Bowater", transporting newsprint paper from Liverpool, Nova Scotia to Alexandria, Washington for the Washington Post and from Corner Brook, Newfoundland to Chicago, with paper for the Chicago Tribune.

Eventually coming ashore, my career progressed through a brief period in wharf management, followed by twenty-five years with one of the leading London firms of cargo surveyors and consultants, Perfect Lambert and Company, where I became a partner. As a surveyor, I was concerned with inspecting cargo and investigating damage claims all over the world, ranging from Patagonia to North Vietnam and most places in between.

Whilst conducting a survey on a small Greek vessel that had been towed into the French port of Brest, following a very serious fire on board, my examination revealed that the engine room of the vessel and the crew accommodation above, had been more or less totally destroyed. The intensity of the fire was such that virtually nothing remained intact, other than a small china egg cup which had miraculously survived, this showing the crest of the original German owners of the vessel.

This I took home as a 'souvenir'. From this small beginning has developed a large collection of shipping company china, not to mention some souvenir items, silver plate, ephemera and glass pieces. My interest in collecting, which had remained dormant whilst I was serving at sea, is not only an act of acquisition, but also one of nostalgia. Every piece I find to add to my collection, brings a visual image of the vessel, where the china was probably used, and the trade upon which the vessels were employed.

Furthermore, my collection has required considerable research into the histories of the more obscure shipping companies, particularly those that existed in the early to mid part of the 19th.Century. This period is my particular interest. Apart from the maritime aspect, there is also considerable pleasure to be obtained in identifying the manufacturers of the china - which has led to further research.

Hartley, Kent   August 2006

ACKNOWLEDGEMENTS

A number of friends and fellow collectors have provided access to their collections and this has given me great pleasure and also increased my knowledge of the subject.

Notably, Laurence & Jennifer Dunn, Gravesend, Kent and Alberto Bisagno of Genoa, Italy, have been particularly helpful. In addition, this book would not have been possible without the computer skills of Kent Tucker, of Hartley. A special thanks is due to Al D'Mello of Wested Press for technical assistance and work on the cover.

All photographs, with the exception of a small number (which are individually credited) are of the Laister collection and were taken by my wife, Pamela. These photographs are only as good as the original china pieces, from which the images were taken. In this respect, the transfer printing on some china is less than sharp, which obviously affects the quality of the final photograph. There are approximately 1,160 coloured photographs, these include images of 615 different items of china. There are also photographs of the crests on the china and illustrations of ephemera and contemporary post cards.

Apart from her talents as a photographer, she has given me her full support in both this publication and acquiring pieces for my own collection. Without her my collection would have been very much the poorer. She has faced many hours of "hunting", frequently in very cold, windy & very wet conditions - always with a cheerful heart - and given me great encouragement when I started to weaken. My debt to her is immeasurable, in all respects.

These two volumes are dedicated to her.

INTRODUCTION

This book is an attempt to illustrate examples of the china used on board British Merchant Ships, and covers the period from the beginning of the 19th.Century, through to the end of the 20th.Century. It also gives brief historical details of the companies themselves, and the trades in which they were involved.

Whilst reasonably comprehensive, no work of this nature, could ever attempt to list all patterns used by any company, nor could it hope to cover all companies, particularly those which only existed for a short period of time in the 19th.Century. Over the period under review, there were literally thousands of different shipping companies, each using a variety of patterns. For the most part the pieces illustrated are of examples from our own collection, and have been acquired over a period of thirty years or so. A few pieces illustrated, are from the collections of friends. Without doubt, many different examples are in the safe hands of collectors scattered around the world, particularly in North America. Many of the collectors domiciled on the Western side of the Atlantic concentrate on the great passenger ship lines, such as the Cunard Steamship Company, White Star Line & French Line etc.

Many different examples of china are already contained in private collections, others pieces await "discovery" and may, given luck, be found in the most unexpected places. This sometimes may be many miles from the sea, and in countries where there is no national, or obvious reason, for their location, as the companies did not trade to the country in which the china was found. This may partially be attributed to ships being sold for breaking up, in countries far from their normal routes. A good example of this is the Italian port of Genoa, where there was a thriving ship-breaking industry at the beginning of the 20th.Century. Other pieces would have been "acquired" over the years as souvenirs!.

The shipping companies covered in these two volumes traded to all parts of the world and, with a very few notable exceptions, are no longer in existence. Some restricted their pattern of trading to coastal waters around the United Kingdom or New Zealand. Others companies traded on a world-wide basis, owning a variety of types of vessels, passenger liners, cargo passenger liners (usually only carrying twelve or less passengers), cargo only and tankers.

Whilst the name "British" is mentioned in the opening paragraph of the introduction, the book also includes shipping companies owned in Australia, Canada & New Zealand etc. These companies were of great importance to the economies of the countries concerned, and to what used to be known as the British Empire.

Many of these shipping companies were essential for the development of the countries and continents to which they traded. Examples are Elder Dempster to West Africa, Pacific Steam Navigation Company to Chile & Peru, British India Steam Navigation Company to the Indian sub-continent, Blue Funnel & Glen Lines to Hong Kong and the Far East, Orient Line to Australia and the New Zealand Shipping Company to New Zealand etc. These prestigious companies formed a link between Britain and her Empire, from the very earliest formative years of the countries.

Without the major passenger carrying lines, such as Cunard, Allan Line and Canadian Pacific to North America, P&O to India & China, Union-Castle to South Africa, Shaw Savill & Albion and New Zealand Shipping Company to the Antipodes, there would have been fewer emigrants, and far from reliable postal services. Expatriates relied on the cargoes and mail brought by sea, as a contact with their home countries.

The book (which is in two volumes) is divided into chapters on a geographical basis and the companies are listed under the chapters appropriate to the area, with which they are most associated. However, it must be remembered that many companies had more than one area of operation. For example, Cunard had services to the Mediterranean and Anchor Line to India. Similarly, whilst Elder Dempster is most associated with West Africa, the company also operated lines both to Canada and the West Indies (Beaver Line and Imperial Direct West India Mail Service Co. Ltd.).

CONTENTS – VOLUME ONE

CONTENTS – VOLUME TWO

TYPES AND SUPPLY OF CHINA

For the most part shipboard crockery had to be strong, durable and capable of withstanding some abuse, either from stewards or the hazards of the sea. During the 19th.Century and through into the 20th.Century, almost all crockery manufactured for shipboard use, consisted of ironstone china (heavy off white earthenware). This was somewhat crude, by comparison to bone china (which was much whiter and finer and which contained between 30% and 50% of bone ash). Bone china was used by some of the more prestigious passenger lines, particularly for 1st.Class passengers. The decoration was usually achieved by applying transfers, sometimes this being enhanced by hand painting, in colour, over the transfers.

In general, the china used on board was similar or identical to that used ashore and was, after all, "hotel ware" that happened to be used at sea. Most patterns & designs were not specifically manufactured for a particular company. Whilst the china was overprinted with the names of the shipping companies, or with their monograms or house flags, identical crockery was often used by more than one line, with the appropriate crest etc. applied. In the case of the cargo or tramp ship owners and, in the lower classes on the passenger liners i.e. 2nd. & 3rd. Class and emigrants, the crockery tended to be plain white/off white. with the name of the company etc. imposed. This type of china was frequently "decorated" with a single coloured band running around the rim of the china, often with a pinstripe running parallel just inside the coloured band, in the same colour. Blue was the favoured colour for such decoration, although the colours red and green were sometimes used. Some companies used both blue or red decoration (an example of this is Houlder Brothers). Another popular embellishment, during the middle part of the 19th.Century, was an anchor chain running around the border of the plate or rim of jugs, usually in a light green or blue colour. A rope border, interspersed with reef knots in a dark blue colour, was also popular, at about the same period of time.

In the case of more decorative china, intricate designs were sometimes favoured and the firm of Minton produced several different designs, these being used by more than one company. An example of this is their 'Key Festoon' pattern, which was used by, amongst others, African Steamship Company, British & African Steam Navigation Company, Elder Dempster, Charente Steam Ship Company (T & J Harrison) and the Chilean line, C.S.A.V. (Compania Sud America de Vapores – Valparaiso).

Another example of a Minton design is their 'Alton' pattern, which was used by the African Steamship Company, Pacific Steam Navigation and Canadian Pacific Railway Company. As in the case of the 'Key Festoon' design, the single colour of light or dark blue was preferred for the decoration.

Particular striking china (bottom marked) was produced by Copeland Spode for Canadian Pacific Steamships and later the Allan Line. This was a 'stock' pattern known as 'Heron' and came in two versions, multi-coloured and blue.

Not all china was top marked, although most collectors prefer items which are nicely marked on the front or top, the bigger the crest, or company name, the better. However, many of the large passenger liner companies, which preferred to use somewhat more sophisticated or bone china in 1st.Class, had their china marked with the company name or crest, on the underside. When the company name was printed on the underside, the manufacturer of the china would charge an extra amount to do so. This was for the copper plate required in the process and for the extra print of the name, which had to be taken off the copper plate. The latter remained the property of the shipping company.

There were a number of ship chandlers, or china and glass suppliers, who specialised in supplying the requirements of the ship owners, such as Stonier & Company, in Liverpool. These suppliers would hold a stock of replacement china in their warehouses, so that when a vessel arrived in port after a poor passage and had sustained a loss of china, due to breakages in heavy weather, the suppliers could arrange to replace the china from stock, within a day or so. This was preferable to having to wait for replacements, to be manufactured.

Apart from Stonier & Company in Liverpool, several chandlers/suppliers existed in the major ports to deal with the ships' requirements. These included Thos. F. Bennett & Company, Eills & Company, Reynolds & Son, R. Livingston, A. B Buxton and D. A. S. Nesbitt & Company (all of Liverpool), Cochran & Fleming, A. Sneddon & Son Limited, Wylie & Lochhead & Sons Limited, McDougall & Sons Ltd., and Christie Brothers (all of Glasgow), McSymons & Potter, (Glasgow & Swansea), C. E. Bevington Ltd., and J. De Fries & Sons, both London, and C. McD Mann & Company, Hanley.

A number of manufacturers, such as Copeland and Davenport, owned their own retail shops and warehouses in the major ports, such as London, Liverpool or Glasgow. Salesmen from these companies would either call at the shipping company's office, or deal with the shipping company's own buyer, when he called at the manufacturers premises, to establish what china was available from stock.

An example of "stock" china, which was used by more than one shipping company, is a Royal Doulton pattern decorated overall with rosebuds, trimmed with a green pinstripe. China of this design was used by the Union-Castle Line, the Royal Mail Lines and the Bank Line. Other examples are a design decorated with flowers, and a tropical bird, used by both the Royal Mail Lines and the Furness Bermuda Line, and a design with small blue flowers overall, used by the Union-Castle Line (later British & Commonwealth) and the British India Steam Navigation Company, in the 1950's'.

Some shipping companies, such as the Orient Line, had their own china specifically designed for them. This company commissioned Wedgwood, and their designers, to produce patterns for their own exclusive use. An important example of this is a stunning pattern of china decorated in purple and black designed by Edward Bawden. This china, with the pattern name "Heartsease", was introduced with the liner "ORONSAY", where it was used in the Silver Grill. Another important pattern was designed by Robert Goodden. This china with a fine earthenware body, was known as "Fouled Anchor" and produced by Wedgwood in their Queensware range, for the P&O-Orient Line in the late 1950's. This was introduced with the liner "ORIANA".

A particularly striking pattern in brown was designed by Edward Bawden and supplied by Wedgwood, exclusively for the New Zealand Shipping Company. This was used in the 1st.Class dining saloons.

Lady Casson designed a new pattern of china for the P&O liner "CANBERRA" in 1961. This was manufactured by Messrs. Geo. L. Ashworth & Brothers and the design consisted of a motif of an endless and intricate maze, in gun-metal grey.

If a shipping company had a pattern, that was exclusive to its own use, it was not uncommon for it to be manufactured by more than one potter. An example of this was china, decorated with seashells in yellow and brown, which was manufactured for the Orient Line in the 1950's and 1960's by Ashworth Brothers, Royal Doulton and the North Staffordshire Pottery Company (Vitrock china).

Whilst most patterns of china were rather plain, understandably so in the case of cargo ship companies and in the 3rd. class and emigrant classes of the passenger liners (the greater the decoration, the greater the cost), some companies in the early part and mid part of the 19th.Century, used very beautiful and ornate crockery. In some instances, the rims of the plates were decorated with flowers and, in the centre, with the portrait of a paddle steamer. Fine examples of these very early pieces are known from the British & American Steam Navigation Company, the Transatlantic Steamship Company, the Eastern Steam Navigation Company (paddle steamer "*PRECURSOR*") and several coastal lines, which operated services between Scotland & London. The latter included the London & Edinburgh Steam Packet Company, London and Edinburgh Shipping Company, Dundee, Perth & London Shipping Company and Dundee & Hull Steam Packet Company.

The Pacific Steam Navigation Company commissioned crockery that was particularly colourful. This was decorated in the centre, in colour, with baskets of fruit and the plates had light blue rims. The china was top marked with the company name, in either English or Spanish, the latter being used on the company vessels employed on the West Coast of South America coastal services, between Panama and Valparaiso, in Chile. The Union Steam Ship Company of New Zealand was another company using very colourful china, decorated with flowers, this crockery being bottom marked.

MANUFACTURERS

The leading potters/manufacturers of the time were employed to produce the china, mostly being well known. Some are still household names in the United Kingdom, although recently a number have shifted their production to the Far East or Eastern Europe, where the cost of labour is much cheaper.

Examples of 19th.Century manufacturers who produced shipping company china are given below:-

John & George Alcock, Corbridge	1839-1846
G. L. Ashworth & Brothers, Hanley	1862-1968 (Mason's Ironstone from 1968)
J & M P Bell & Co. Ltd., Glasgow	1842-1928
Edward F Bodley & Co. (or Son) , Burslem	1862-1898
Booths Limited, Tunstalll	1891-1948 (later Booths & Colclough Ltd.)
Sampson Bridgwood & Son, Longton	1805 -
Brown-Westhead, Moore & Co., Hanley	1862-1904
Clementson Brothers, Hanley	1865-1916
Copeland & Garrett, Stoke	1833- 1847
Copeland W.T. & Sons Ltd., Stoke	1847 (now Copeland Spode)
Davenport, Longport	1793-1887
Doulton & Co., Lambeth etc.	1858-1956
Dunn Bennett & Co., Burslem	1875 -
James Edwards & Son, Burslem	1839-1841
Thomas Hughes, Longport, Burslem	1895-1957
Johnson Bros. (Hanley) Ltd	1899-
Kerr & Binns, Worcester	1852-1862
M. King, The Pottery, North Shields	
John Maddock & Sons Ltd., Burslem	1855 -
C. T. Maling & Sons Ltd., Newcastle upon Tyne	1890-1963
Mann & Company, Hanley	1858-1860
Minton, Stoke on Trent	1793 -
Francis Morley & Co., Shelton, Hanley	1845-1858
John Ridgway & Co., Shelton, Hanley	1830-1855

Ridgwood, Morley, Wear & Co, Shelton, Hanley 1836-1842
Wedgwood & Co. Ltd., Tustall   1860-1965
James F Wileman, Longton   1869-1892
Arthur J Wilkinson Ltd., Burslem   1885-1947
F. Winkle & Co. Ltd, Stoke on Trent   1890-1931

In addition to some of the potters listed above, who produced china in both centuries, the following companies manufactured shipping company china in the 20th.Century :-

William Adams & Sons (Potters) Ltd., Tunstall & Stoke 1769-
Adderleys Ltd, Longton   1906 -
Chas. Allertons & Sons, Longton   1859-1942
John Aynsley & Sons Ltd., Longton   1875 -
Bakewell Brother Ltd., Fenton   1927-1943
E. Brain & Co. (Foley China), Fenton   1903-1963
British Anchor Pottery Co.Ltd., Longton   1884-
Cauldon Limited, Shelton, Hanley   1905-1920
George Clews & Co.Ltd, Tunstall   1906-1961
Dudson Bros. Ltd., Hanley   1898-
Furnivals Ltd., Corbridge   1890-1968
Gibson & Sons Ltd.,Burslem   1885-1985
Grindley Hotel Ware Co.Ltd., Tunstall   1908-
Hammersley & Co.   1887-
Jackson & Gosling Ltd., Longton   1886-1961
A B Jones & Sons Ltd., Longton (Royal Grafton) 1900-1972
Keeling & Co. (Losol Ware)   1886-1936
J & G Meakin Ltd., Hanley   1851-
Myott, Son & Co. Ltd., Corbridge & Hanley   1898-
North Staffordshire Pottery, Corbridge & Hanley (Vitrock) 1940-1952
R H & S L Plant Ltd., Longton (Tuscan China) 1898-
Pountney & Co. Ltd ., Bristol   1849-1969
Ridgway Potteries Ltd., Stoke on Trent   1955-1964
James Sadler and Son Ltd., Burslem   1899-
Royal Doulton formerly Doulton, Lambeth   1882-
Josiah Wedgwood & Sons Ltd., Burslem   1759-
H . M. Williamson & Sons, Longton   1879-1941

These potters were for the most part situated in the Stoke on Trent area of the English Midlands, "The Potteries".

Dating and Identification

Dating and identifying china used on board ships can be very frustrating and covers the full spectrum, from easy to difficult, if not impossible. Most collectors have a box hidden away, where pieces accumulate dust, pending identification. Some of these may turn out to be treasures, most are likely to be of no interest.

Of course, the easiest pieces to identify are those bearing the name of the company, or a company house flag, and from a collectible point of view these are the most desirable. However, even if the pieces are marked in this way, it can still be difficult to learn much about the company, when the china dates from the 19th.Century. This is especially the case, if the company only survived for a year or so..

Books of House Flags

Books detailing shipping company flags and liveries are essential tools. Of these, three books published by Lloyds of London are the most invaluable, when dealing with early pieces. These books, Lloyd's List of House Flags published in 1882, and Lloyd's Book of House Flag & Funnels published in 1904 and 1912, are themselves very collectible. Contemporary to these, are books published by Griffin & Company, Portsmouth - "Flags National & Mercantile House Flags & Funnels", and by Thomas Reed & Co. Ltd., Sunderland. In the case of the latter publisher, their "S. S. House Flags" and "Reed's Flags and Funnels" are of particular use, when dealing with the more obscure cargo ship and tramp companies of North East England.

Other more recent books are those published by Brown, Son & Ferguson, Ltd, Glasgow, "Brown's Flags & Funnels", which now runs into nine editions, and "Flags, Funnels and Hull Colours" published by Adlard Coles Limited.

The Liverpool Journal of Commerce published a number of Charts depicting House Flags & Funnels, over a period of several years. Two other noteworthy books on the subject are "House-Flags and Funnels of British and Foreign Shipping Companies", drawn and edited by E. C Talbot-Booth in 1937 and " A Survey of Mercantile Houseflags & Funnels" by J. L. Loughran, published by Waine Research Publications in 1979. This book also gives interesting details concerning the shipping companies, and how their house flags evolved.

All the above are helpful, but unfortunately there are many companies which are not recorded, this being particularly true of the early 19th.Century lines and the less prestigious companies.

Date & Registration Marks

Date & registration marks on the china are also invaluable, but rarely appear ; White Star Line china in the first decade of the 20th.Century was sometimes marked with the month and year, as was Cunard Steamship Company ivory ware china, manufactured by John Maddock & Son. Other more recent pieces carry an impressed date mark.

A diamond shaped mark was impressed, or printed, on Victorian china between 1842 and 1883. These marks recorded the class of china, the day of the month, the month, the year and parcel number. From 1884 registered designs were numbered consecutively, with the prefix "Rd" or "Rd. No". Again, this information is invaluable, with the proviso that it is only one part of the equation. For example, the dates and numbers show when the design or pattern was first registered. However; some patterns, like Minton's "Key Festoon", were used over several decades and could give a false impression, as to when the china was in use by the Shipping Company. That is, the design was registered, before the shipping company came into existence

Apart from the above, many of the leading manufacturers had their own system of date marks and these can also be of great assistance, provided you are aware of the system they adopted.

Undoubtedly the most invaluable source of information, when it comes to china marks, including dates, is the "bible" of collectors, the "Encyclopaedia of British Pottery and Porcelain Marks" by Geoffrey A. Godden, published by Barrie & Jenkins. This details, and illustrates, many of the marks used by china manufacturers, both large and small. It is very comprehensive, nevertheless, even this great work cannot illustrate all the marks and variations which occur.

An indication as to date of manufacture can also be obtained, when the marks give the name "England" or "Made in England", The former was added to marks from 1891 and the latter indicates a 20th.Century date. This, however, does not always hold true, as Ashworth Brothers continued to show the mark "England" into the 20th.Century, and not the latter mark.

Monograms

Without doubt, china that is top marked with a monogram or intertwined letters can be the most difficult to identify, unless the monogram is surrounded by the company title, usually in a garter. An example of this is the "CNCCo" monogram used on early china, by the China Navigation Company. Given the absence of the shipping company name, or a house flag, on the piece, one has to resort to deduction, which can be all too fallible. In this situation, company literature or letterheads can be the answer to the collectors dilemma, as frequently the same monogram or logo is used, on both the tableware and written material, such as letterheads or brochures.

Named vessels

For the most part, ships tableware was not marked with the name of a particular vessel, it just did not make economic sense to do so. Retaining a stock of "named" china, in a warehouse, was a costly business, particularly for companies whose vessels carried a large number of passengers. Like all generalizations, however, there were exceptions; and in the 19th.Century a number of companies had very ornate china manufactured for them. This bore the name of the ship, and sometimes a portrait of the supposed vessel, usually a paddle steamer. These "portraits" were, to say the least, often inaccurate and frequently contained a large amount of artistic license.

As the years elapsed and the shipping companies became controlled more and more by accountants, rather than by "shipping" people, many stopped using marked china and relied on "off the shelf" purchases, of stock patterns. There were honourable exceptions to this and most of the remaining prestigious passenger liner and cruising companies still have china, either designed for them, or top or bottom marked with their name, or logo. P&O, until recently at least, commissioned china that was marked with the name of the vessel i. e., " *CANBERRA*", "*ORIANA*" etc.

In the case of other vessels, china was specially manufactured for the ship when she was built. An example of this, is a pattern which resembled gold "snowflakes". This was used by the Cunard Line on the "*QUEEN ELIZABETH 2*", when she was brought into service. In some companies, special china was commissioned for specific dining areas on the vessels, such as Grill Rooms. Here the passengers were charged a supplement for the pleasure of dining in more elegant surroundings, or receiving extra special care and attention. An example of this was very striking china, with a rich blue border, which was manufactured by Copeland Spode for the grill rooms of the White Star Line vessels "*OLYMPIC*" and "*TITANIC*". Pieces of this china are very hard to find and command very high prices, when they come on to the market. Other examples of "exclusive" china were to be found in the Queen's Grill of the "*QUEEN ELIZABETH 2*" and the grill rooms of the Orient Steam Navigation Company's liners, already mentioned.

China printed with the name of specific vessels was not confined to the passenger liner companies. Many of the more mundane shipping companies, such as the owners of cargo liners, tramp ships and colliers provided their vessels with china, which bore the name of the vessel. Almost invariably this china was plain, being decorated at the rim with one or more coloured bands (usually blue, sometimes red) and the name of the vessel. This china was sometimes marked with a house flag, within a garter or similar surround.

Some indication as to, where and when, tableware was used and on which ships, i. e. what class and period of time etc., may be established by studying official postcards and brochures. These were issued by the shipping companies to illustrate the dining areas on their vessels. Regrettably some of these illustrations, whilst depicting the dining saloons, are not clear or sharp enough to determine the patterns on the china, or show empty tables. Nevertheless, it is always worth checking these illustrations. Communicating with the few remaining ship owners requesting information about china patterns, and when in use, is rarely productive, as the individuals who would have known are no longer with us. Also, company records from the earlier years are either non-existent, or contain scant information.

Unfortunately, china patterns are sometimes attributed to a specific class, or vessel, when the provenance of this attribution, which may be based on false premises or speculation, cannot be relied upon. This is particularly so in the case of earlier pieces of china, dating from the 19th.Century. With modern vessels, however, such as the *"QUEEN ELIZABETH 2"* the china patterns are well documented and company literature and other pieces of ephemera and books are profusely and clearly illustrated with photographs, showing the dining areas on board, and the table settings.

<u>Prices</u>

No prices are given in this work, as to some extent prices are meaningless and can fluctuate, both up and down. This is because prices are dependent on a number of variable factors, such as supply and demand and whether or not companies are "fashionable", at the time etc. Clearly pieces from the 19th.C are harder to come by and understandably command higher prices.

Recently on line auctions and in particular eBay, have changed the market considerably, both to the advantage and disadvantage of the serious collector. The internet has opened up the world to collectors, so that later, and more common pieces, are easier to come by. This has to some extent depressed the prices of such pieces. Even the prices of White Star Line china have come down somewhat, from the very high prices and the buying frenzy that prevailed, after the film "Titanic" was released. On the other hand, serious collectors now have the opportunity of acquiring rare and older pieces "on line", although the competition for these pieces is usually fierce.

CHAPTER 5   **India, Burma and the Far East**

Asiatic Steam Navigation Company

Bibby Line

Blue Funnel Line (Alfred Holt & Company)

Bombay & Bengal Steamship Company Limited

British India Steam Navigation Company Limited

Thos. Jno. Brocklebank Ltd.

Calcutta & Burmah Steam Navigation Company Limited

China Navigation Company Limited

Eastern Steam Navigation Company

Glen Line Limited

Henderson Line (and the Irrawaddy Flotilla Company)

Peninsular & Oriental Steam Navigation Company (P&O)

ASIATIC STEAM NAVIGATION COMPANY

A British cargo liner company founded in 1878 and re-constructed in 1931. The company was managed by Turner and Company, London. The vessels were employed on the coast of the Indian sub continent serving such ports as - Calcutta, Rangoon, Akyab and coast ports to Bombay & West India via Ceylon, Java ports to Burma, Coromandel, Calcutta, Ceylon, Malabar, Bombay, Kathiawar and Karachi, Calcutta to Rangoon , Madras & Port Blair. The officers were British and the crew lascars. Most vessels carried a small number of passengers

Left illustration, an egg cup by Dunn Bennet; right a soup plate with double rope border in blue by Stonier/Bridgwood.

Rectangular comport with double rope border in blue with additional green floral decoration over the glaze. E. F. Bodley & Son Circa 1881 and the manufacturers mark..

The company was later taken over by the British India Steam Navigation Company, thus becoming part of the P&O Group.

BIBBY LINE

The Bibby Line was formed in Liverpool in 1807, by John Bibby, in association with John Highfield. The two partners commenced regular sailings to Dublin from Parkgate on the River Dee. Shortly after this they started sailings to the Baltic, South America and the Mediterranean. The latter became the most important area of the company's operations for a number of years, although it was with Burma that the Bibby Line became most associated in its more recent history.

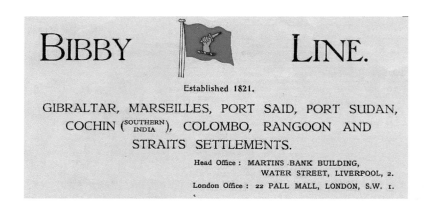

The transition from sail to steam began in 1850, by which time the company had become John Bibby & Sons (the Bibby family owning the company from its inception through to the present time). The iron screw steamer RATTLER of 276 grt was built in 1846, followed by the ARNO 660 grt and the TIBER, both built in 1851, and a number of other vessels.

Dinner plate by Cauldon Rd.64182 Circa 1887 supplied by Thos. F. Bennett & Co., Liverpool. Note the original plain red house flag, to which the Bibby family crest of a hand grasping a sword or dagger was added late in the 19th.Century.

Gradually the trade to the Mediterranean and in particular to Alexandria diminished in importance and several vessels were transferred to the North Atlantic trade to Boston. This was apparently at the suggestion of Frederick Leyland, who had become a partner in the Bibby Line in 1859. From 1873 until 1889 the firm came under the control of the Leyland Line, but returned to the Bibby family in 1889. With the opening of the Suez Canal in 1869, trade to the East became of greater interest to the Victorian shipowners and the area was generally well served by companies such as P & O, British India, Anchor, Clan, City and Brocklebank. The Bibby Line felt there was more potential for a service to Burma, where competition was less, other than that from the City and Henderson Lines.

Soup plate recovered from the wreck of the Bibby Line vessel BRAGANZA off the Welsh coast. Back marked W. James & Son, Liverpool and the Liver Bird detail on the front.

The above illustration shows a soup plate recovered from the BRAGANZA (1856/507 grt) which was wrecked off the Welsh coast in 1869. Examination of a painting of the ARNO of 1851 reveals her to be flying a white flag on her foremast, which clearly depicts a black Liver Bird. However, the Bibby Line are unable to confirm one way or the other whether the soup plate came from her table service, or whether it came from her cargo, as she was carrying a consignment of china at the time of her loss.

Side plate supplied by Stonier & Co., Liverpool and detail of crest.

In 1888 an order was placed with Harland & Wolff, Belfast; for two larger steamers, the LANCASHIRE (1889/3,870 grt) and YORKSHIRE (also 1889) to be employed on the Burma trade. These were followed by the CHESHIRE (1891/5,708 grt) & SHROPSHIRE (1891/5,721 grt). The naming of the Bibby Line ships after English counties starting with the LANCASHIRE, continued until the company ceased owning vessels.

Apart from Passenger and cargo services, the Bibby Line became heavily involved with the carriage of troops. This commenced with the YORKSHIRE, which was chartered by the British Government to take troops to the Boer War in October 1899, culminating with the OXFORDSHIRE (1957/20,586 grt). This vessel was more or less similar in size and appearance to the British India troopship, NEVASA. The OXFORDSHIRE was sold to Sitmar Line in1964 and became the FAIRSTAR.

Egg cup Circa 1938 supplied by D. A. S. Nesbitt & Co. and milk jug by Maddock & son.

The Bibby Line vessels had a very distinctive appearance with a single tall pink, black topped funnel; the later motor vessels were graced with larger funnels than those that were the norm for other companies. Most of the early vessels had four masts.

Variations in style – ornate, early part 20thC. and "modern".   Cube shaped hot water jug by Grimwade.

The company was the first to introduce the "Bibby Cabin", which became common to many other liner companies before the widespread use of air conditioning and verandah cabins. The system consisted of a block of four cabins, two pairs in an "L" shape, so as fully utilize all space but to permit a porthole in each cabin, essential in hot climates.

In 1965 the company decided that the passenger service to Rangoon and Colombo was no longer economically viable, and the two vessels on the service at that time, the WARWICKSHIRE (1948/8,903 grt) and LEICESTERSHIRE (1949/8,908 grt) were withdrawn, thus ending a service, which apart from wartime, had continued since 1891. The company still exists, for the most part being involved in storage and distribution, having diversified latterly into bulk carriers, liquefied gas carriers and even accommodation barges; one at least, the BIBBY VENTURE, being used as a floating detention facility in New York, where no doubt the inmates were treated somewhat differently to the first class passengers to Rangoon during the company's heyday.

Plain white chamber pot with line name & company crest in brown supplied by D. A. S. Nesbitt & Co.

China was usually front marked with the Bibby Line name in a ribbon and the family crest as illustrated. The suppliers were the well known Liverpool firms, Stonier & Company and D. A. S. Nesbitt, both of these companies supplying tableware to many of the Liverpool based shipowners.

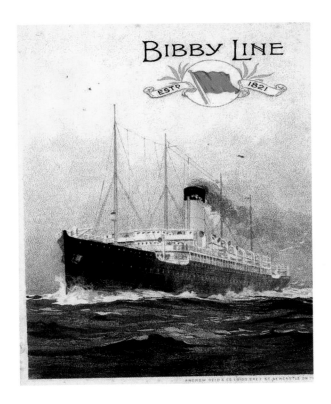

Company post card showing the traditional Bibby Line four masts.

BLUE FUNNEL LINE
(ALFRED HOLT & COMPANY)

THE BLUE FUNNEL LINE

ALFRED HOLT & CO., LIVERPOOL.

FIRST-CLASS PASSENGER SERVICES FROM LIVERPOOL TO

**MARSEILLES, PORT SAID,
THE STRAITS and CHINA**

London Passengers are conveyed to Liverpool by Special
First Class Train on Sailing Day at the Company's expense.

REDUCED SUMMER FARES :—

SOUTH OF FRANCE, EGYPT & PALESTINE.

MARSEILLES.—Special Summer Return £22, from April to September.
Passengers may travel by Sea both ways, or by Sea one way and Train
the other.

PORT SAID.—Special Summer Return Fare from the U.K. from
24th May to 16th August, and returning not later than 1st December
from Egypt, £35.

T.S.S. SARPEDON.

The Ocean Steam Ship Company was founded in January 1865, by Alfred & Phillip Holt. Alfred Holt was trained as a locomotive engineer and for a number of years had been investigating the possibility of "compounding" engines, that is making them more fuel efficient and economical to run. Prior to the commencement of Ocean Steam Ship Company, Alfred Holt had acted as an engineer consultant and tried out compound engines on the CLEATOR The results of these trials confirmed that it would be viable to steam to the Far East. Accordingly, Alfred & Philip Holt decided to commence services to China and three vessels designed by Alfred Holt were ordered in 1865 from Scotts of Greenock. These were the AGAMEMNON, AJAX and ACHILLES, each of approximately 2,200 grt.

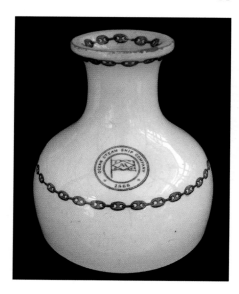

Large ironstone water jug by G. L. Ashworth top marked "Ocean Steam Ship Co.1866".

From the beginning the vessels bore names after mortals in the Iliad and Odyssey of Homer. Because of their blue, black topped funnels (of very large and imposing dimensions) the company was known to seafarers as "Blue Flue". The fleet invariably consisted of sturdy well managed vessels, whose scantlings were in excess of those required by Lloyds Register and the classification societies. The ships were largely self insured by the company.

In 1883, weekly sailings commenced to the Malay States, Malacca Straits and China. In 1890 a joint fortnightly service was started between Singapore and Java to Fremantle, this beginning a long standing connection with Australia. A wholly owned Dutch subsidiary, the Nederlandsche Stoomvaart Maatschappij 'OCEAN', was formed in 1891 to develop trade with the Dutch East Indies. The vessels on this service continued the Homeric naming system and the familiar blue funnels.

Competition arrived on the scene in 1882/1884 in the shape of the "The China Shippers Mutual Steam Navigation Company", a company set up to serve the interest of the shippers of cargo, rather than the shipowners. This very active competition was dealt with in 1902, when Ocean Steam Ship acquired China Mutual Steam Navigation Company and, with that company, a new service between China and the West Coast of the United States of America and Canada.

Large bowl by Ashworth circa 1880, with the name "China Mutual Steam Navigation Co."

Whilst the company was essentially interested in cargo, the original three vessels carried some forty cabin passengers; and in 1910 three vessels were built with accommodation for some 200 or so saloon passengers These were the AENEAS, ANCHISES and ASCANIUS, each about 10,048 grt.,- for the Australian trade. Two larger vessels with similar passenger capacity were built in 1913, the NESTOR and ULYSSES, each 14,500 grt.

Rectangular bowl from the passenger service, "Avondale" pattern by Copeland Spode Rd .No .637555 circa 1918.

152

Side view of comport and Johnson Brothers detail.

Two cargo liner companies were acquired to replace tonnage lost in the 1st.World War, the Indra Line in 1915 and the Knight Line of Steamers in 1917. However, by far the most important company to come under the umbrella of the Ocean Steam Ship Company was the Glen Line in 1935, together with the Shire Line, following the collapse of the Royal Mail Group. The same year a controlling interest was obtained in the Straits Steam Ship Co., providing services from Singapore to the Malay Straits.

A very fine coffee cup & saucer supplied by Stonier & Co. Ltd., Liverpool.

Examples of coffee cups & saucers.

153

A rare example of china marked with the house flag on the top, supplier, Eills, Liverpool and a cream coloured oyster dish, also top marked.

In 1936 the Ocean S.S.Co had become the largest shareholder in Elder Dempster Line Holdings (the main British cargo liner shipowners to West Africa) and the sole shareholder in 1965. The fleets became fully integrated with vessels frequently interchanging between Blue Funnel/Glen and Elder Dempster as and when required. Full integration of Elder Dempster within the group only took place in 1967, at which time the honourable name of Alfred Holt & Co. disappeared.

The most common Blue Funnel china manufactured by Ashworth Brothers and supplied by Eills, Liverpool circa 1950's.

In 1972 the firm of William Cory & Sons, (collier and tug owners) was taken over and the name Ocean Steam Ship Company changed to Ocean Transport & Trading Company Limited. So yet another famous name in the British shipping industry was no more.

An example of china used by the Ocean Group in its latter days. The bottom mark on the right is that of the Ocean Steam Ship Company, prior to the name change in 1972 to Ocean Transport & Trading. The china illustrated above was sometimes bottom marked with the company name and house flag in black, or with the name "Blue Funnel and Glen Line" and was used on board both Blue Funnel & Glen Line vessels.

To all intents and purposes, the Ocean Transport & Trading Company ceased to be shipowners in March 1989, when Elder Dempster sold its interests to the French Group, Delmas Vieljeux. In 1970 Ocean Transport & Trading owned more than 100 cargo liners. By 1976 this had dropped to 45 vessels and by 1989 to a single vessel, a gas carrier.

The company crest used on menus and writing paper circa 1930's.

BOMBAY & BENGAL STEAMSHIP COMPANY LIMITED

The Bombay Steam Navigation Company was founded in 1846, and by the mid part of the 19th.C the Bombay & Bengal Steamship Company Limited was operating in the Calcutta to Rangoon trade.

A very rare warming plate used by the Bombay & Bengal Steamship Company. The purple colour of the decoration is unusual, the more common colour being dark blue or green. The manufacturer is unknown.

The company was in direct competition with the British India Steam Navigation company on the through route. Further details concerning this line are not recorded.

BRITISH INDIA STEAM NAVIGATION COMPANY LIMITED

In the days of the very powerful British Empire, several liner companies dominated the trade between the home country and the Indian sub-continent. Of these, one of the most important was the British India Steam Navigation Company (B.I.S.N.); known to all and sundry as "B.I.". This company provided coastal services around the Indian Coast, as well as liner services between the sub-continent and East Africa, the Persian Gulf and to Great Britain and later to Japan and Australasia. The company was founded in 1856 by William Mackinnon, of Messrs. Mackinnon, Mackenzie and Company, together with London investors, as the Calcutta & Burmah Steam Navigation Company Limited to run a mail service between Calcutta and Rangoon.

The company's first two vessels were the CAPE OF GOOD HOPE of 500 grt built in 1856 for the General Screw Company's service between London and South Africa and the BALTIC of 535 grt, built by Messrs. Thomas Wilson in Hull, for their own service to the Baltic (the Wilson Line), in 1854.

Examples of the company crest used on china.

In 1862 William Mackinnon obtained a subsidy from the Government of Bengal, following a proposal he made to operate a scheduled service calling at every port between Calcutta & Karachi. As a result, the British India Steam Navigation Company was officially registered on the 28th.October 1862. After a protracted negotiation with the Dutch Government, the Netherlands India S.N. Co. (Nederlandsche Indische Stoomboot Maatschappij) was set up in 1886 to extend the company's service to Singapore and to operate within the Dutch East Indies. The vessels on this service were required to be registered under the Dutch Flag. This company survived until 1891, when it was taken over by the Dutch K.P.M. Line. British India Associated Steamers (B.I.A.S.) was formed in 1876 to manage the vessels that were not based in India, the B.I.A.S. steamers being owned by shareholders. This company was wound up in 1903.

Throughout its long history "BI" was involved in trooping and both the CAPE OF GOOD HOPE and BALTIC were used as troop transports during the Indian Mutiny. During other periods of strife the company continued to provide troop transports and obtained Government Trooping contracts. Trooping was continued until 1962.

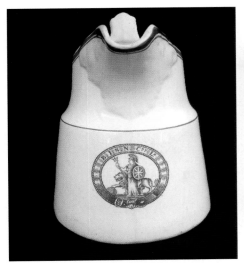

*Large milk jug by Wilkinson Limited and a coffee cup & saucer showing
the combined flags of the Union Steam Ship Company of New Zealand, British India, P & O and the New
Zealand Shipping Company. These were used on china circa 1920, after P & O took the companies over
during the First World War.*

On 17th.November 1869 the Suez Canal was opened and "BI" commenced a liner service between India and the United Kingdom. (the "Home" service), and trunk lines from the U.K. to the Red Sea & Persian Gulf ports. Any service commencing from a British port was designated a "Home Line" and managed initially from Glasgow - later London - as opposed to "Coast Lines", which were based in either Calcutta or Bombay.

In 1872 a monthly mail service was commenced between Aden & Zanzibar, the vessels connecting at Aden with steamers on the direct service between the U.K. and India. This service eventually developed into the numerous East African lines operated by "BI", culminating in the East African Mail service, the largest vessels of which were the KENYA (1951/14,434grt) and her sister, the UGANDA of 1952.

The latter eventually became a "School Ship." Later as a Hospital ship she earned her place in history during the Falklands conflict, being chartered in 1983 by the Ministry of Defence to operate between Ascension Island and Port Stanley, in the Falklands.

*The vegetable dish is marked "British India Steamers".   The tea pot with Blue flowers overall is circa
1950's (the same pattern was also used by Union-Castle).*

Tea pot side marked with crest, decorated at the rim with blue "arrows" and a small milk jug (both manufactured by Ashworth Brothers).

During 1914 "BI" and P & O amalgamated. The two companies had co-operated harmoniously in the past, but the amalgamation was not obvious as the two companies retained their separate identities and services. This situation continued until 1971 when the P & O SN Co. was divided into Passenger, General Cargo and Bulk divisions. The "BI" cargo vessels were quickly transferred into the new cargo division and painted in a new corporate livery.

The last "BI" passenger vessel in line service was the DWARKA (1947/4,851grt), which was employed on the Bombay-Persian Gulf line. She was broken up in 1982 still in her "BI" colours, consisting of the famous black funnel, with two white bands. The "BI" livery was, however, retained on UGANDA until 1986 when she was towed to Taiwan for breaking up, although by this time she was under P & O ownership.

For the most part the company's china was marked with Britannia holding a trident, standing alongside a lion with its fore foot on a globe. Beneath Britannia was a scroll encompassing the initials B.I.S.N., although some of the older pieces bore the company name in full. Silver plated and glass items were marked, for the most part with BISN Co. in a belt with a buckle. Some pieces of glassware were marked with the full company name and Britannia.

Terracotta milk jug bottom marked with both the "BI" and P & O initials.

THOS. & JNO. BROCKLEBANK LTD.

The Brocklebank Line can claim to be one of the oldest shipping companies in the world, tracing its history to 1770 when Daniel Brocklebank established a ship-building business in New York. As a direct consequence of the American War of Independence Brocklebank returned to the North of England, where he had originally been born, and initially started trading as a shipowner with the small brig CASTOR. In 1785 he commenced as a shipbuilder in Whitehaven, many of the vessels built by the yard sailing under the Brocklebank house flag. Daniel Brocklebank was joined in the family business by his sons, Thomas and John. In 1801 the founder died, the firm then taking the name Thos.& Jno. Brocklebank, a name that prevailed throughout the remainder of the company's existence until 1968.

An early soup plate used by the company with house flag detail.

For the most part, in the formative years, the vessels traded to North & South America and the West Indies. However, following the collapse of the Honourable East India Company and their monopoly, the first Brocklebank vessel was dispatched to Calcutta in 1813, this marking the start of their services to India for which the company became famous. Until 1889 all sailings were conducted by sailing vessels but that year saw the introduction of the first steam powered vessel, the AMEER (4,127grt) built by Harland & Wolff, Belfast.

Coffee cup & saucer supplied by Stonier & Company, Liverpool & a coffee cup & saucer showing the house flag, as depicted in the 1960's.

In 1907, a half share was acquired in the Shire Line of Steamers which gave the company an opening in the Calcutta – Far East trade, this share being given up to The Royal Mail Steam Packet Company in 1911. In the same year, the line became associated with the Cunard Steamship Company and the Anchor Line, Anchor-Brocklebank Ltd. being formed in 1912. The Well Line of Sunderland (Tysack & Branfoot) was taken over in 1916, which allowed access into East Coast ports and also to Colombo & Madras on the East coast of India.

Examples of manufacturers and suppliers marks.

Thos. & Jno. Brocklebank remained part of the Cunard Group throughout the ensuing years, Cunard-Brocklebank Ltd. being formed in 1968, Cunard Brocklebank Bulkers Limited in 1972. The final pair of ships were disposed of in 1983. For the most part the company's power driven vessels bore names such as MAIDAN, MAHSUD and MAGDAPUR etc. and the company was unusual in that the blue & white house flag was flown on the foremast, rather than on the mainmast.

Built in 1815, the ship " Princess Charlotte ", 514 tons, served the company for 30 years. She carried the Brocklebank houseflag into the Bay of Bengal and beyond the Java Sea

CALCUTTA & BURMAH STEAM NAVIGATION COMPANY LIMITED

The Calcutta & Burmah Steam Navigation Company Limited was founded on 24th.September 1856 by William Mackinnon of Messrs. Mackinnon, Mackenzie and Company, together with London investors, to run a mail service between Calcutta and Rangoon. The company was registered in Glasgow.

The company's first two vessels were the CAPE OF GOOD HOPE of (1876/500grt) built for the General Screw Company's service between London and South Africa, and the BALTIC of (1854/535grt), built by Messrs. Thomas Wilson in Hull for their own service to the Baltic (the Wilson Line).

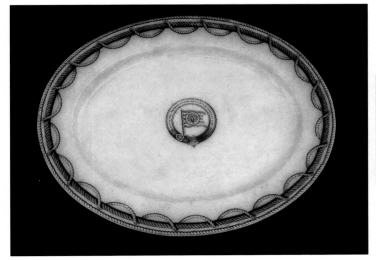 

Large ironstone platter supplied by Mann & Co., Hanley.

Note the Burmese Peacock used on the company china (a very similar emblem was used by the Irrawaddy Flotilla Company on their china).

In 1862 William Mackinnon obtained a subsidy from the Government of Bengal, following a proposal he made, to operate a scheduled service calling at every port between Calcutta & Karachi. As a result the company was renamed and officially registered as the British India Steam Navigation Company on the 28th.October 1862.

CHINA NAVIGATION COMPANY LIMITED

The China Navigation Company was founded in 1872 as a Yangtze River company, although the parent company, John Swire & Sons Limited, dates from the beginning of the 19th. Century. In 1865 Alfred Holt, an engineer who was interested in forming a direct steamer service to the Far East, which later evolved into the great Ocean Steam Ship Company (Blue Funnel Line), approached his friend John Samuel Swire seeking investment in his new company.

Crest of the China Steam Navigation Company as shown on earlier patterns of china.

John Swire & Company already had an interest in the Far East, where the company was represented by an agent, with whose services they were not entirely satisfied. John Swire agreed to take an investment in Holt's new line and was offered the Ocean Steam Ship Company's agency, an agency that was to have great endurance and continued for many years. John Samuel Swire proceeded to Shanghai in 1866 where he set up his own agency under the name of Butterfield & Swire; Butterfield being a UK based partner in the new venture (although Butterfield left the company after a few years, the name of Butterfield and Swire continued to be used). The Swires considered that a Yangzte River service had great potential, not least as a feeder service for the Ocean Steam Ship Company. However, Holt was not interested and the Swires decided to set up the China Steam Navigation Company on their own account, in conjunction with several leading Liverpool firms.

The China Navigation Company purchased an existing river company, the Union Steam Navigation Company, in 1872 and it's two steamers the TUNSIN & GLENGYLE; and ordered three new paddle steamers the PEKIN, SHANGHAI and ICHANG, from Glasgow shipbuilders. These vessels arrived in Shanghai in 1873 and the new line prospered and formed the nucleus of a company that has endured to this day.

Early platter by G. L. Ashworth & Brothers, circa 1880.

The political situation in China was such that the company decided Hong Kong would be a more suitable location for their head office. At Hong Kong they became one of the leading merchant houses (setting up an office in India during the period when Hong Kong was occupied by the Japanese army, during the Second World War). Apart from ship owning, Butterfield & Swire had interests in the Taikoo sugar refinery, Taikoo Dockyard, the insurance industry and also Cathay Pacific Airways.

The Yangzte River services extended to the upper, middle and lower reaches of the river, as far inland as the city of Chungking and through the rapids of the Upper Yangzte Gorges. The company also operated regular passenger services on the China Coast, to the Malay Straits, the Philippines, Java, Japan, Australia & New Zealand. In 1953 they began operating a Straits-Jeddah Hadj service, carrying Muslim pilgrims en route to Mecca.

Serving dish – manufacturer unknown and later crest.

At the beginning of the 21st.Century the company is still actively involved in shipping services around the Pacific Rim, with modern vessels of all types. It also operates four ex. Russian built multi purpose vessels on a round the world service (these previously being owned by the Bank Line).

EASTERN STEAM NAVIGATION COMPANY

The Eastern Steam Navigation Company was set up with the express intention of operating steam ships to India; the gentlemen involved were nicknamed the "Precursors". This was because they claimed to be the first to put forward the idea of such a service. Another company set up at the same time was the East India Steam Navigation Company, the persons behind this being nicknamed the "Comprehensives". The latter proposed to run steamers between Egypt & Ceylon and, from there, comprehensive services to Bombay & Calcutta. The cost of setting up these services was very high and P&O proposed that both companies should amalgamate with P&O, a proposal that was accepted by the "Comprehensives" but rejected by the "Precursors", who had the wooden paddle steamer PRECURSOR built. (1841/1,751grt).

A warming plate manufactured for the Eastern Steam Navigation Company's PRECURSOR, "New Japan Stone" china manufactured by Copeland & Garrett circa 1841..

The Eastern Steam Navigation Company never became operational and failed to carry out any voyages. The PRECURSOR was sold to P&O in 1844 for £45,000, to become their 24th. Vessel. She was reduced to a hulk at Suez in 1858 and broken up in 1869.

The underside of the warming plate was marked with the manufacturer's name, the name of the vessel and "Eastern Steam Navigation Company." The banner on the mast also shows the name of the vessel.

GLEN LINE LIMITED

One of the most prestigious passenger/cargo liner companies operating services from the United Kingdom to the Far East, the Glen Line was founded in 1869 by James McGregor, who was a partner in the firm of Alan C. Gow & Company. The first vessel to carry a "GLEN" name was the GLENAVON (1868/1,080grt), a sailing ship which was employed on a service from Glasgow to Calcutta, Singapore, Penang and other ports in the Far East.

The first Glen Line steamer was the GLENGYLE (1870/1,614grt), which was built for the China tea trade to London, a port that became the head office of the company.

In 1880 James McGregor became the senior partner and the name of the firm was altered to McGregor, Gow & Company. The Glen Line Ltd. was formed in 1910 and in the following year all of the Glen Line shares were purchased by Elder Dempster & Co. Ltd. This company had been taken over by Owen Phillips, of the Royal Mail Steam Packet Co. in 1910, so that Glen Line effectively now became part of the R. M. S. P. "Group".

Company name on a soup plate. Supplied by Hutton & Co. West India Dock Road, London, East.

This led to a joint venture with the Shire Line, that had been bought by the Royal Mail Steam Packet Co. (who were, by 1909, beneficial owners and by 1911 full owners of Shire Line). Both companies had already worked amicably on services to the Far East, so that the inauguration of a joint service made good sense. The name Glen & Shire Line was introduced in 1920. During the First Word War six ships were lost through enemy action, all the Glen Line vessels being fast and large cargo carriers of a very high standard, some with accommodation for 12 passengers.

Saucer with grey/green decoration at the rim and bottom mark showing the company house flag. China used in the later years of the company was bottom marked..

By 1929 the vast Lord Kylsant/Royal Mail group, that included such illustrious names as White Star Line, Elder Dempster & Union-Castle as well as the Royal Mail and Glen & Shire Lines, was in deep financial trouble which led to a total collapse in 1931. Glen & Shire Lines were purchased by Alfred Holt & Company (the Blue Funnel Line) in 1935. From thence the histories of both Glen Line & Blue Funnel became interwoven, to such an extent that vessels were sometimes exchanged between the two companies, carrying the appropriate GLEN or Blue Funnel name & livery.

Milk jug manufactured by Ashworth Brothers, supplied by Eills, Liverpool who also supplied china to Blue Funnel .

During the Second World War Glen Line vessels, which had advanced design, speed and range, were employed on Malta Convoys, converted into Landing ships, commissioned as H.M. Auxiliary Supply Ships or converted into Escort Aircraft Carriers. Three ships were lost.

The name of the owning company was changed to Ocean Transport & Trading Ltd. In 1972, and the fleets of Glen Line, Blue Funnel and Elder Dempster (which was by this time wholly owned by Alfred Holt) came under the name, Liner Shipping Limited. Containerisation was now the order of things and the days of conventional cargo vessels were numbered. The Ocean group was no exception to this and by 1977/78 all "Glen" Line vessels had been sold and no vessels were owned by the company. However,the Glen Line name still existed, being bought by Curnow Shipping of Porthleven, Cornwall in 1990

HENDERSON LINE
(& The Irrawaddy Flotilla Company)

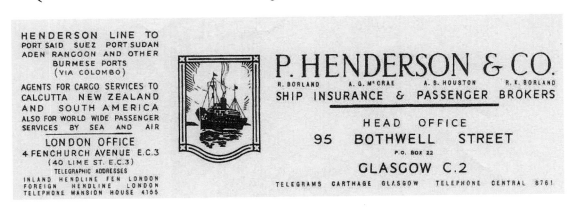

HENDERSON LINE TO PORT SAID SUEZ PORT SUDAN ADEN RANGOON AND OTHER BURMESE PORTS (VIA COLOMBO)

AGENTS FOR CARGO SERVICES TO CALCUTTA NEW ZEALAND AND SOUTH AMERICA ALSO FOR WORLD WIDE PASSENGER SERVICES BY SEA AND AIR

LONDON OFFICE
4 FENCHURCH AVENUE E.C.3
(40 LIME ST. E.C.3)
TELEGRAPHIC ADDRESSES
INLAND HENDLINE FEN LONDON
FOREIGN HENDLINE LONDON
TELEPHONE MANSION HOUSE 4155

P. HENDERSON & CO.
R. BORLAND   A. G. McCRAE   A. S. HOUSTON   R. K. BORLAND

SHIP INSURANCE & PASSENGER BROKERS

HEAD OFFICE
95 BOTHWELL STREET
P.O. BOX 22
GLASGOW C.2

TELEGRAMS CARTHAGE GLASGOW   TELEPHONE CENTRAL 8761

Whilst the Henderson Line (or Paddy Henderson's as it was familiarly known) is best remembered for its trade to Burma, the Henderson Brothers first became involved in shipping in 1835, when a vessel was chartered by them to carry the firms own goods between Italy & Scotland. This was notably for the import of marble from Leghorn. By 1838 George Henderson owned two vessels under the name of Patrick Henderson.

By 1848 large numbers of people were emigrating from Scotland to New Zealand and the Hendersons chartered sailing vessels for this trade. In 1852 the Albion Line came into being. The first settlers in a company "owned" vessels sailed on the LADY DOUGLAS in 1856 and the Albion Shipping Company was registered in 1864.

The Irrawaddy Flotilla Company was formed in 1865 to serve the inland waters of Burma; As Patrick Henderson & Company saw potential growth in the Burmese trade, they commenced routing some of the homeward bound sailing vessels from New Zealand via Burmese ports.

Direct sailings from Europe to Burma were envisaged from 1870, and the British & Burmese Steam Navigation Co Ltd was formed in 1874, although the company's first steam powered vessel, the TENNASSERIM (1871/1,837grt) made the first sailing a couple of years or so before the company was actually founded.

The company's involvement in the New Zealand trade ceased in 1882 when the Albion Line amalgamated with Shaw, Savill to form Shaw, Savill & Albion, although the company's trade to Burma flourished. A serious competitor entered the trade to Burma in 1889, when the Bibby Line commenced a service from Liverpool to Burma. However, the two lines decided to co-operate and it was agreed that the British & Burmese S. N. Co. would concentrate on sailings from Glasgow & Liverpool, the Bibby Line from Liverpool & London.

In 1893 the frequency of sailings to Burma was increased, which left the company with a shortage of vessels. Accordingly a "joint" company was formed, together with James Spencer of Glasgow who injected 50% of the capital, the remaining 50% being held by Hendersons. All the shares in this company, the Burmah Steam Ship Co. were acquired by the British & Burmese S. N. Co in 1934.

A very fine egg cup from the S. S. CHITTAGONG (1881/1,912 grt) circa 1881. This vessel was owned by P. Henderson as opposed to the British & Burmese S. N. Co. and built by Raylton Dixon & Company Middlebrough.

Throughout the first half of the 20th.Century the line continued to operate passenger and cargo liner services to Burma, losing four vessels during the First World War and six in the Second, including one marine casualty.

By the beginning of the Second World War the Irrawaddy Flotilla Company dominated the inland waterways of Burma, owning approximately 650 craft of all types, including large passenger carrying paddle steamers. However, the fleet was decimated in 1942, either by bombing or scuttling as an act of denial, following the Japanese invasion of Burma. Upon cessation of the war, the fleet was quickly re-built, only to become nationalised in 1948 when Burma became an independent state.

In 1952 Elder Dempster Lines Holdings purchased all shares of the British & Burmese S. N. Co Ltd. At this time four vessels were trading to Burma and management of these remained with P. Henderson. Six vessels that were not required by the Henderson Line were already on charter to Elder Dempster. In 1953 the group became Liner Holdings Ltd. (the major shareholder being the Ocean Steam Ship Co. Ltd (Alfred Holt/ Blue Funnel). All shares in Elder Dempster and the Henderson Line were purchased in 1965, by the Ocean Steam Ship Company.

The imposing crest of the Irrawaddy Flotilla Company Limited used on the company china. A covered tureen manufactured by Dunn, Bennett & Co. (Royal Vitreous Pottery).

Cream coloured tea plate decorated with red, green & black pinstripes used by both the Henderson Line and Elder Dempster Lines in the 1960's

The Six Day Arab war closed the Suez canal in 1967, and this marked the end of the Henderson Line involvement with Burma. By 1970 the one remaining British & Burmese S. N. Co vessel was sold and yet another well known name in British shipping was no more.

The Irrawaddy Flotilla Company name, however, was resurrected in 1995 by the author & historian Paul Strachan and now operates two "up-market" vessels on cruises up the Irrawaddy and Chindwin rivers.

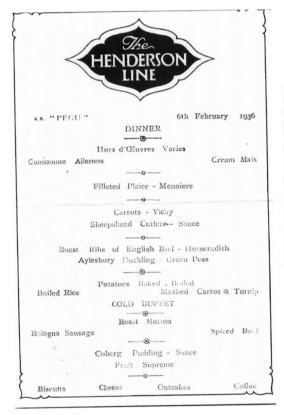
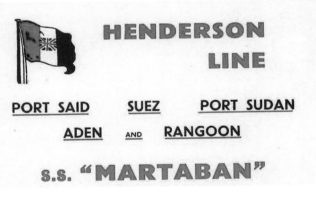

Dinner menu from the PEGU 1936 and a sailing notice from the MARTABAN circa 1960.

PENINSULAR AND ORIENTAL STEAM NAVIGATION COMPANY

The great Peninsular & Oriental Steam Navigation Company (P&O); is without doubt one of the most famous names in British shipping and one of the few companies that have survived into the 21st Century.

The company has its origins in a steamship service from Falmouth to Oporto, Lisbon, Cadiz and Gibraltar that started in 1825 with the small steamer WILLIAM FAWCETT. The company name refers to the Spanish peninsula; The two principal partners of Brodie Willcox and Arthur Anderson were involved at this time with trade to both Portugal and Spain and supporters of the Royal families of both countries. This connection is still perpetuated as the colours of the P&O house flag, red, yellow, white & blue were the colours of the national flags of Spain & Portugal.

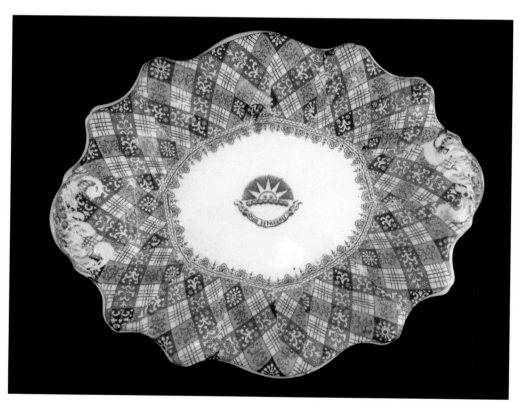

This is the first known pattern of ironstone china used by the company and was manufactured by Ridgeway, Morley & Wear circa 1846.

The "sunburst" has been used in various forms on crockery and paperwork from the beginning of the company. The illustrations show the manufacturers mark "Caledonian" pattern and Victorian registration mark.

In 1837 the partners obtained a contract to carry mails as far as Gibraltar, where they were transferred to Admiralty packets for carriage onwards to Alexandria. The company name at this time was the Peninsular Steam Navigation Co. In 1840 the partners commenced operating their own vessels as far as Egypt. At Alexandria the mails were taken overland to Suez for the onwards journey to Bombay, India by East India Company vessels. The same year, the name of the company was changed to Peninsular & Oriental Steam Navigation Company, reflecting the interest in the Orient. It was incorporated by Royal Charter on the 1st.December 1840, with its articles including India and the Far East.

The overland route across Egypt became very famous and at first was very arduous. P&O had their own farms to provide food and their own rest camps etc. Whilst initially all camels and equipment for the route were provided by the Pasha, these services were found to be inefficient. Accordingly, by 1844 these requirements were taken over by P&O themselves. An auxiliary branch of the company was set up, the Egyptian Oriental Transit Company. As a matter of interest, some 3,000 camels were required to carry baggage and mails for one small vessel.

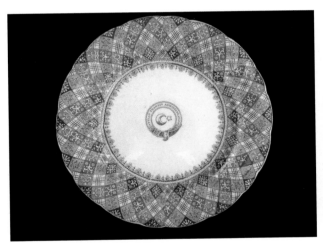

China, also in the "Caledonian" pattern, thought to be used on the Overland Route.

The first P&O vessel to operate east of Suez was the HINDOSTAN (1842/2,018grt) which left Southampton on the 24th. September 1842 for Galle (Ceylon) and Calcutta. A contract was obtained from the British Government to convey mail in the area of Suez, Ceylon, Madras & Calcutta in 1842, and in 1844 a mail contract was awarded to the company for a service from Ceylon to Penang, Singapore & Hong Kong. This was followed in 1852 by a mail contract to cover the route from Singapore to Australia. The same year also saw the company carrying the mails from Suez to Bombay, previously the monopoly of the Honourable East India Company.

Very early plate by John Ridgway & Co. circa 1840.

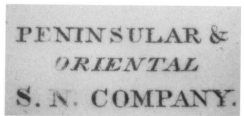 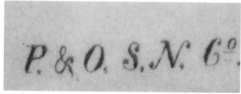

Bottom marks from china of the design above.

P&O played its part in the service of the country in the Crimean War in 1854-5, and transported some 60,000 troops and 15,000 horses during this conflict. A further 6,000 men were transported during the course of the Indian Mutiny a few years later. This service to the crown has continued through all major (and minor) wars since, many ships having been involved in trooping, carrying supplies or serving as Armed Merchant Cruisers. One of the most well known of these was the passenger liner RAWALPINDI (1925/16,697grt) which was sunk by the German battleships SCHARNHORST and GNEISENAU in 1939, whilst defending a convoy. These conflicts led to the loss of many fine vessels, both cargo and passenger.

Well ant tree meat plate made by Ashworth Brothers, circa 1862.

The Suez Canal was opened in 1869 and, whilst the P&O vessels were able to use the canal, the Admiralty insisted for a further four years that all mails were sent overland across Egypt and reloaded to a vessel at Suez, for on-carriage to their destination.

Fruit bowl by F. Morley & Co. circa 1860

In fact, the opening of the canal caused serious problems for many ship owners, and in particular P&O, as many of their vessels had been built specifically for service between England and Alexandria and from Suez to the Orient and were unsuitable for the longer direct voyage. This situation was aggravated for P&O by the large amount of capital that had been invested in the Overland Route.

The manufacturers marks for F. Morley & Co. and Ashworth Brothers.

Thomas Sutherland was Managing Director of the company in 1872 and he took the bold decision to rebuild the fleet with more suitable vessels, and eleven new ships joined the fleet in 1873. This was followed by further new vessels over the ensuing years. In 1887 four ships were built to mark the Golden Jubilees of both Queen Victoria and the Peninsular & Oriental Steam Navigation Company itself. These "Jubilee" ships were the VICTORIA (6,522 grt) and BRITANNIA (6,525 grt), both built in 1887, and OCEANA (6,610 grt) and ARCADIA (6,603 grt), both built in 1888.

Dinner plate by Copeland circa 1860 and double ended egg cup with a blue "moorish" design, internally marked at both ends with the company crest in blue.

Chamber pot by Bakewell Brothers. The rope design/crest was used from the latter part of the 19thC. until the early decades of the 20th.C

In 1910 the fleet and goodwill of William Lund's Blue Anchor Line was acquired. This company had long operated routes to Australia via the Cape of Good Hope, largely in the emigrant trade and had recently lost the steamer, WARATAH, which had disappeared without trace off the South African coast. The five vessels taken over with the Blue Anchor Line, were soon replaced by P&O with five new vessels, all of which carried names beginning with the letter "B" e. g. BALLARAT (1911/11,120grt). The new service became the "P&O Branch Line" to Australia.

The first of many acquisitions by P&O took place in 1914, when the Australasian United Steam Navigation came under the company's control. The same year an amalgamation was agreed between P&O and the British India Steam Navigation Company. In 1916 the New Zealand Shipping Company and the Federal Steam Navigation Company were acquired, followed in 1917 by the Union Steamship Company of New Zealand, the Nourse Line and the Hain S. S. Company. A majority shareholding was acquired in the Khedivial Mail Line and a majority interest in the Orient Line. The Eastern & Australian Mail S.S. Co was acquired in 1919. Other purchases were the General Steam Navigation Company in 1920, the Strick Line in 1923 and the Moss-Hutchison Line in 1935.

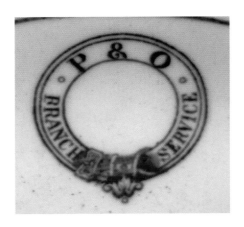

P&O Branch Line crest.

A total of nineteen P&O vessels (plus a large number of vessels from the group and associated companies) were lost during the 1914-18 war and, as in earlier conflicts, the company's liners were occupied as Armed Merchant Cruisers, Hospital ships or Troopships and Transports. A large fleet replacement programme of both cargo and passenger vessels commenced upon cessation of hostilities. These included the liners MOOLTAN (1923/20,847grt), the first P&O vessel to exceed 20,000 tons and VICEROY OF INDIA (1929/19,648grt), the first passenger ship with turbo-electric propulsion.

Jardiniere manufactured by Royal Doulton circa 1920.

In the 1920's, china , glass and paperwork was produced showing the P&O "sunburst" and the combined house flags of the Union SS Co. of NZ, British India, P&O and the New Zealand Shipping Co.

Terracotta jug bottom marked for use by both P&O and the British India S. N. Co.

Five large STRATH liners were built in the 1930's, STRATHNAVER (1931/22,270grt), STRATHAIRD (1932/22,544grt), STRATHMORE(1935/23,580grt), STRATHEDEN(1937/23,732grt) and STRAHALLAN (1937/23,722grt). All five ships were taken up as troopships during the Second Word war and the STRATHALLAN was torpedoed and sunk in 1942, the other four liners surviving.

Very simple china was used in the latter part of the 1930, through to the 1960's. This was cream coloured & decorated with red, green & blue pinstripes The manufactures were Bakewell Brothers and Ashworth Brothers.

Chamber pot by Ashworth Brothers.

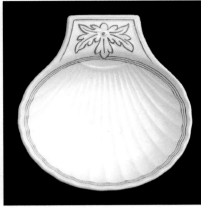

Tea pot used to serve China tea made by Ashworth ; & butter dish by Bakewell Brothers.

The immediate post war years saw a major replenishment programme and a number of war built standard vessels were acquired for the cargo fleet, as well as new buildings. As far as the passenger fleet was concerned, the world had already begun to change with more passengers travelling by air (a process that accelerated with the arrival of jet aircraft). Nevertheless, four new liners were built, commencing with the HIMALAYA (1949/27,955 grt,) thence the CHUSAN (1950/24,215 grt), ARCADIA (1954/29,664 grt) and IBERIA (1954/29,614 grt. A new transpacific service, named the Orient & Pacific Line commenced in 1958 and P&O-Orient Lines was formed in 1960 to manage both the P&O and Orient Line passenger vessels. The following year saw the introduction of the CANBERRA (1961/45,270 grt), designed for the Australian service to run as a partner to the new Orient Line liner, ORIANA. The CANBERRA was an innovative vessel and at first experienced a number of machinery problems. In 1973/4 she was converted to full time cruising and became a much loved and long lived vessel in this role. As passenger numbers fell off the other new liners were also used for cruises, cruising eventually becoming an important part of P&O' s business. In fact, in the early years of the company, holidays to the Mediterranean had been promoted by the company and in 1904 the redundant liner ROME (1881/5,013 grt) had been converted for full time cruising and renamed VECTIS. During the inter war years many surplus liners were also used for this purpose.

China was specially designed for the CANBERRA by Lady Casson and manufactured by Ashworth Brothers. The tea pot would have been used for serving China tea.

The year of 1965 was an important one for P&O, as the minority shareholding in the Orient Line was acquired and the two "fleets" fully integrated. Sadly, the Orient Line name was dropped in 1966 and the same year P&O joined with Alfred Holt/Blue Funnel Line, British & Commonwealth and Furness Withy to form the consortium of Overseas Containers Limited (OCL).

At this time, containerisation of cargo was in its formative stage, but within a few years it would have a very large impact on the carriage of cargo. This caused the demise of a large number of conventional cargo liners of all companies, including those in the P&O Group. The P&O General Cargo and Bulk Shipping Divisions were formed in 1971 to operate the group's cargo vessels and the vessels of British India, Strick Line and the New Zealand Shipping Company etc. were transferred to the new divisions (losing their identity and proud names in the process).

The SPIRIT OF LONDON (1972/17,370 grt) was purchased on the stocks in 1972, the first passenger vessel owned by P&O that was built specifically for cruising. She was renamed SUN PRINCESS, when the company acquired the American line, Princess Cruises in 1974. In 1988 a further cruise line came under the P&O umbrella, the Monaco based Sitmar International, P&O then becoming one of the largest companies in the cruise market.

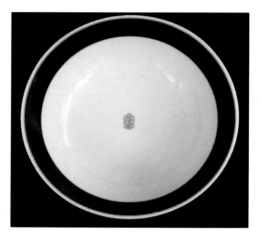

Large bowl by Royal Doulton decorated with a broad royal blue band at the rim and with the P&O Coat of Arms in gold in the centre. This coat of arms was granted to the company in 1937, its centenary year. Up until then the Latin motto used was "Quis Separabit", being changed when the Arms were granted in 1937 to "Quis Nos Separabit".

New liners joined P&O Cruises, amongst them a "new" ORIANA (1995/69,153 grt) and the AURORA (2000/76,152 grt) which were built with the British market in mind (Princess Cruises being more inclined to the American market) and the cruise lines were de-merged in 2000, to become P&O Cruises and P&O Princess Cruises PLC.

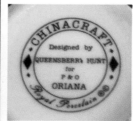

China was made especially for the CANBERRA & ORIANA, by Wedgwood and Chinacraft

China specially designed for the OCEANA and CANBERRA, manufactured by Chinacraft and Steelite International.

The various member companies of Overseas Containers Limited were all bought out by P&O and the name P&O Containers adopted. This part of the company merged with the Dutch company, Nedlloyd and became P&O Nedlloyd Containers, being taken over in 2005 by the Danish company, Maersk Line. Sadly, although P&O remains one of the few survivors of the once numerous British ship owners; the Group has diversified into road transportation, warehousing, logistics and the operation of ports in various parts of the world, it is a mere shadow of the great shipping company that it was in earlier times.

The three cruise lines, P&O Cruises, P&O Princess Cruises and Swan Hellenic are now owned by the American owned Carnival Corporation, although the P&O Cruises vessels still sail under the British flag, as do the remaining vessels of the P&O Ferries division.

In 2006 what remained of the group was acquired by DP World, Dubai's state owned Ports, Customs & Freezones Authority.

Contemporary Post Card of the CALEDONIA (1894/7558 grt).

CHAPTER 6   **Australia and New Zealand**

Aberdeen Line (Aberdeen & Commonwealth Line)

Australian Commonwealth Line

Australian Pacific Mail Steam Packet Company

General Screw Steam Shipping Co.Ltd.

Lund's Blue Anchor Line

New Zealand Shipping Company Limited

Orient Steam Navigation Company (Orient Line)

Panama, New Zealand and Australian Royal Mail Company

Port Line (Commonwealth & Dominion Line)

Shaw Savill & Albion Co.Ltd. (Shaw Savill Line)

Union Steam Ship Company of New Zealand Limited

ABERDEEN LINE & ABERDEEN & COMMONWEALTH LINE

GEO. THOMPSON & C°

ABERDEEN & LONDON.

The Aberdeen Line was begun by Mr. George Thompson in Aberdeen in 1825 and from the beginning was famous for the quality of its vessels. Initially the company traded with sailing ships to London & Quebec, although by 1840 the line was known in most major ports of the world. The vessels were famous for their green hulls and this colour scheme was carried through to the later steam driven ships.

For much of the line's history the most important service was to Australia, where the trading name "Aberdeen Line" was well established. It was also known as the Aberdeen White Star Line because of the white star in the company house flag.

The best known of the sailing ships was the THERMOPYLAE, although other well known ones were the CENTURION, PATRIARCH and MILTIADES etc.

The first steam vessel was the ABERDEEN (1881/3,616 grt), although the most famous of the powered vessels was the JERVIS BAY of the Aberdeen & Commonwealth Line. She was sunk as an armed merchant cruiser by the German heavy cruiser ADMIRAL SCHEER on the 5th.November 1940.

Crest used on the early company china & detail of dinner plate recovered from the bottom of Port Phillip Bay, Melbourne, Australia.

Aberdeen & Commonwealth Line was formed in 1928 after the Australian Government company "Australian Commonwealth Line" was taken over, George Thompson and Co having become a public limited company in 1905, the White Star Line and Shaw Savill & Albion being shareholders.

In 1932 the Shaw Savill & Albion Line took over the Aberdeen Line, which had become involved with the Kylsant empire that had collapsed in 1931. In 1936 Furness Withy took over Shaw Savill, including the Aberdeen Line, the company finally ending in 1957.

Examples of the china used by the Aberdeen Line are illustrated below, some pieces being decorated in red and some in blue. The manufacturers were William Legg & Dunn Bennett.

Coffee cup & saucer for the Aberdeen & Commonwealth Line with a black crest & a chamber pot, both supplied by C. McD Mann & Co.

Manufacturers mark and Aberdeen & Commonwealth Line bottom mark.

— Starting. —

Emigrants on the MARATHON.

AUSTRALIAN COMMONWEALTH LINE

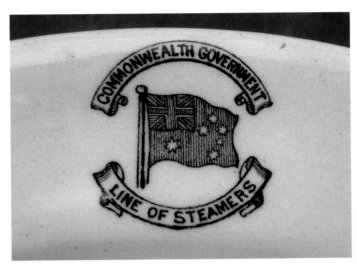

Details of crest as depicted on company china.

In 1916 the Australian Government formed the Commonwealth Government Line of Steamers, partially to ensure that the Commonwealth had adequate vessels to serve the country's trade, as most British vessels were involved on war service, and partially because the government felt that the line would be very profitable.

The line was renamed the Australian Commonwealth Line in 1923, five passenger vessels being built in the United Kingdom in 1921-22. These were the MORETON BAY, LARGS BAY, HOBSONS BAY, ESPERANCE BAY and JERVIS BAY.

In the event the line was very un-profitable, largely because of the high labour costs incurred by using Australian crews. The ailing company was taken over by the White Star Line in 1928, who formed the Aberdeen and Commonwealth Line the same year, the managers being George Thompson & Company of the Aberdeen Line, to which please refer.

AUSTRALASIAN PACIFIC MAIL STEAM PACKET COMPANY

Company crest on a dinner plate manufactured by F. Morley & Co. Circa 1854.

The Australasian Pacific Mail Steam Packet Company was incorporated by Royal Charter on the 9th.October 1852, following a meeting convened by the chairman of the Royal Mail Steam Packet Company in April of that year with directors of the Pacific Steam Navigation Company (P.S.N.C.).The intention or hope was that a trans-Pacific liner service could be operated and managed by the P.S.N.C. to link up with the Royal Mail Steam Packet Co. service to Panama, thus forming a through service from Great Britain to Australasia. Orders were placed for five iron screw steamships, the KANGAROO, EMEU, BLACK SWAN, DINORIS and MENURA. However, the company never commenced the trans-Pacific service and the EMEU and KANGAROO were chartered for Government transport service and the three other vessels were sold to the French company, Messageries Imperiales, Paris. The company was wound up following a meeting in May 1854, apparently due to a number of factors e.g. coal prices for bunkers, the onset of the Crimean War and the lack of a Government mail contract.

Very rare half pint mug.

Whilst the Trans-Pacific line never commenced services the company commissioned china in at least two colours, china with black decoration and another service with blue decoration, both illustrated above.

185

GENERAL SCREW STEAM SHIPPING CO.LTD

The company was formed in 1848 and took over a business that was already trading to the Netherlands. A route to the Levant soon followed and in 1850 the company tendered for and won the Cape Mail contract. An extension to India and Australia was envisaged and several large iron auxiliaries were commissioned. These vessels, the QUEEN OF THE SOUTH, INDIANA, LADY JOCELYN, CALCUTTA & MAURITIUS, were all of approximately 1850 tons. Two more vessels followed.

Large platter used on board the General Screw Steam Shipping Company steamers supplied by Jonathan Phillips 358 & 359 Oxford Street, London (Bisagno collection).

The inaugural sailing to Australia was commenced by the iron steamer HARBINGER on the 11th.February 1853, followed by the HELLESPONT two weeks later. Sailings to Australia were thence carried out on a somewhat intermittent basis by a number of vessels, until October 1854.

However, by late 1854 the company was in serious financial difficulties and in 1856 it was decided to sell eight of the company's vessels to a French concern. This sale was not completed and in 1857 the eight steamers were transferred to the European and American Steam Shipping Company. The General Screw Steam Shipping Company was finally liquidated in April 1862.

The ARGO, a sailing vessel with auxiliary steam power.

LUND'S BLUE ANCHOR LINE
(Wilhelm Lund & Co)

Wilhelm Lund was born in Apenrade, Denmark (part of the German Duchy of Schleswig) in 1837. He commenced seafaring when he was twenty years old and soon developed a fascination for Australia, which influenced him in his future career as a ship owner.

He moved to London in 1860 and his first vessel as a ship owner in his own right, was the wooden barque AMBASSADOR (1869/71 grt). She was the first of seven barques or ship rigged sailing vessels to be owned by Lund and traded on the company's triangular route, outwards with passengers and cargo to Australia, the vessels then proceeding in ballast to China, where they loaded cargoes of tea for the voyage home to Europe.

The first steamer owned by Wilhelm Lund was the DELCOMYN (1880/1,817 grt) which was built for the London to Australia service, via Cape Town. She was followed by the YEOMAN and the HUBBUCK, the latter being the first of several similar three masted vessels.

A chamber pot, clearly showing the Lund's Line white house flag, with a blue anchor. This flag was displayed on the ships black funnels.

At this time the predominant cargo from Australia was wool, passengers being few in number and incidental to the carriage of freight. By 1890 the company had commissioned seven steam ships and the decision was taken to dispose of the remaining sailing ships and concentrate on powered vessels. These were mostly given Aboriginal names. By 1894 there was a demand for refrigerated space to carry increasing shipments of meat and fruit from Australia. Several vessels were, therefore, fitted with refrigerated compartments, later vessels being built with refrigerated cargo chambers already installed.

In 1895 there was a great need for berths for emigrant passengers, sparked off by the discovery of gold. To meet this need, Lund ordered three sister vessels with accommodation for 50 1st.Class passengers and provision for the carriage of large numbers of emigrants. These were the NARRUNG (1896/5,078 grt), WAKOOL (1898/5,004 grt) and WILCANNIA (1899/4,953 grt).

Regular sailings to Australia had to be suspended between 1899 and 1901, as Lund's vessels were used to transport troops to the Boer War. This service to the crown consisted of the carriage of horses from England to Cape Town and horses and supplies from Australia to the Cape.

By 1904, Lund's Line owned five passenger carrying vessels and one cargo ship and operated a monthly passenger service from London to Australia, which alternated with the Aberdeen Line. The same year the line became a limited liability company, Blue Anchor Line Limited.

The last and largest vessel to be built for the company was the ill-fated WARATAH (9,339 grt). She was built by Barclay Curle in 1908 and sailed on her maiden voyage to Australia in November of the same year. She left Adelaide on July 7th. 1909 homeward bound on her second round voyage and called at Durban on the 25th.July, leaving there for Cape Town on the 26th. July. After this she was never seen again, other than being sighted by the Clan Line vessel, CLAN MACINTYRE, on the morning of the 27th.July.

An exhaustive search revealed no trace of her, there were no signs of wreckage, and where she sank together with her complement of 211 passengers and crew, still remains one of the great mysteries of the sea. It was thought in 2005 that her remains had been found on the South African coast, but this was later discounted. An official enquiry was held in London in 1910 to investigate the circumstances of her loss and suggestions were raised about her stability and, in particular, that she may have been "top heavy", although as she had taken coal bunkers and fresh water at Durban this seems to have been unlikely. The most probable cause of her loss was that she ran into a very severe storm on the 29th. July and foundered as a result.

A contemporary post card of the ill fated WARATAH.

The loss of the WARATAH led to the demise of the Blue Anchor Line and in January 1910 P&O acquired the goodwill of Lund's Blue Anchor Line, together with its five remaining passenger vessels. Blue Anchor Line went into voluntary liquidation in July of the same year.

P&O converted the five vessels to carry third class passengers only and at first they were operated as a separate entity, within the P&O fleet. This service later evolved into the P&O Branch Line to Australia. Five larger vessels were ordered to replace the ships transferred from Lund's Line and these were given Australian place names beginning with the letter "B".

Until 1914 the Blue Anchor Line house flag was retained on the funnels of the ships employed on the Branch Line Service. However, the vessels were then given black funnels and all signs of the Blue Anchor Line disappeared.

THE NEW ZEALAND SHIPPING COMPANY LIMITED

One of the great "British" passenger & cargo liner companies, the New Zealand Shipping Company was formed in New Zealand in January 1873 by a group of local business men. These had met the previous year in Christchurch to discuss their concern that the trade, from and to New Zealand, was dominated by "overseas " lines, e. g. the Albion Line & Shaw Savill Line.

Initially the new line operated with chartered sailing vessels, although two ships were purchased in the formative year, the HINDUSTAN which became the WAITARA and the DUNFILLAN which became the MATAURA. Their new names reflected the system of nomenclature for all the company vessels, which were given Maori names.

At this time the company was heavily involved with the carriage of emigrants and remained so for many years. The N.Z.S. Co.'s first venture into the carriage of frozen meat, which was to be of great importance to the economies of both New Zealand and the line, occurred in 1882 after a dry air refrigeration system was fitted into chambers on the MATAURA. This vessel sailed from Port Chalmers (Dunedin) in April 1882 with frozen carcasses of mutton, plus a few sides of beef and pigs that were discharged in London in good order.

The route to New Zealand from the "Home Country" is one of the longest in the world and as the early engines required a considerable amount of coal bunkers, which led to a reduction in cargo capacity, steamers were not a viable proposition without the subsidy of a mail contract. A mail contract was finally given to both the New Zealand Shipping Company and Shaw Savill & Co. in 1883 and the New Zealand. Shipping. Co. built their first three steamers, the TONGARIRO, AORANGI and RUAPEHU, all of 4,163 grt.

A close working relationship was maintained with the Shaw Savill Co. for many years.

The company house flag depicted on early china. The sailing vessels flew this flag, however, with the introduction of steamers a tri-colour pennant was flown above the flag, when the vessels were proceeding under both sail and steam. This steam cornet was shown on later china and advertising material.

A half - pint mug by Alfred Meakin circa 1914 showing the full house flag of the company with the "steam" pennant.

Dinner plate by Royal Doulton circa 1917 showing the company crest in the centre and, most unusual, a monogram on the top rim.

The New Zealand Shipping Company took over the Federal Steam Navigation Company in 1912, with its twelve steamers named after English Counties e. g. DEVON. From that date much of the company china and literature showed the crossed house flags of both companies. The crest on the china was in green or blue and, sometimes in full colour, and in full colour on promotional literature.

An event of great moment to the company took place in 1916 when the P & O Steam Navigation Company acquired both the N.Z.S Co. and Federal Lines, although for the time being, management of the vessels remained with the two companies.

Rectangular platter showing the flags of various P&O companies by Ashworth Brothers circa 1920.

China and glassware was introduced circa 1920 showing the "sun burst" of P&O and the house flags of the New Zealand and Federal companies and also British India and the Union Steamship Company of New Zealand, both of the latter companies being owned by P &O.

Soap dish from a compactum by Dunn Bennett & Co. showing the crossed house flags in blue.

Dinner plate with a blue border by Dunn Bennett circa 1922 and house flag & pennant in green.

This full coloured house flag complete with tri-colour pennant or "steam cornet" was shown on china ranging from egg cups to chamber pots.

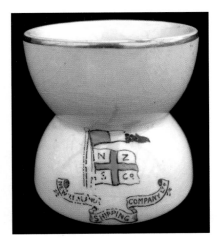

Chamber pot by George Jones Crescent China and an egg cup with a gilt rim.

In 1929 the company introduced three two funnelled passenger motor ships, the famous RANGi's,, the RANGITIKI, RANGITATA and RANGITANE all of approximately 16,700 grt. The two former vessels survived the Second World War and continued on the passenger service to Wellington via the Panama Canal until 1962. The RANGITANE, was, however, sunk by the German raiders, ORION & KOMET in November 1940.

China for use on the passenger vessels was especially designed for the company by Edward Bawden in the 1950's, (who also designed china for the Orient Line). It was manufactured by Wedgwood & Company and used in 1ˢᵗ.Class.

Other china supplied by Wedgwood was plain "Celadon" and light green in colour.

From the beginning of the New Zealand Shipping Company's ownership of steamers the vessels had a livery which consisted of a black hull, with a pale cream funnel. This continued until 1966, when the funnel colour of all vessels was changed to that of the Federal Steam Navigation Company, a red funnel with a black top with their red, white & blue house flag superimposed on the red.

Dinner plate with house flags in green by Ashworth Brothers circa 1950's.

In 1971 the company's cargo vessels were transferred to the newly formed P&O General Cargo Division, together with other constituent members of the group e. g Hain Line and Strick Line etc. In 1973 the P&O livery of a mid blue funnel, with a deep corn coloured hull was adopted fleet-wide

The final vessels to carry New Zealand Shipping Company names were the cargo vessels TAUPO (1966/10,983 grt) and TEKOA (1966/10,975 grt), albeit with the colours of the Federal S. N. Co. These vessels were sold in 1980 and this marked the end of the New Zealand Shipping Co., after one hundred and eight illustrious years on the very long trade route to New Zealand.

ORIENT STEAM NAVIGATION COMPANY

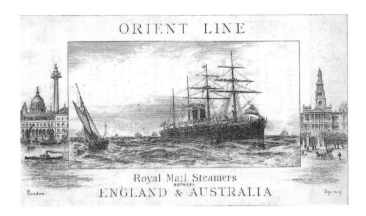

One of the most prestigious British passenger liner companies, the Orient Steam Navigation Company was registered in the year 1878 by Messrs. Anderson, Anderson & Company, in conjunction with Frederick Green & Co., using four surplus steamers purchased from the Pacific Steam Navigation Company. Of these vessels, three, the LUSITANIA, CHIMBORAZO and CUZCO had carried out voyages on charter a year earlier to establish whether the new line would be a viable proposition. The fourth, the GARONNE, had been delayed and a Dutch vessel, the STAD AMSTERDAM, had been chartered as a substitute. Apart from the partners, the Pacific Steam Navigation Company (PSNC) was a heavy subscriber to the new company.

However, the Orient Line had actually started regular sailings to Australia with the three masted barque ORIENT (1,033 grt) in 1866 under the name Orient Line of Packets to Australia and already placed two chartered steamers on a voyage to Melbourne in 1874.

Initially the service was on a monthly basis and a "back up" vessel, the ACONCAGUA was chartered from PSNC to fulfill this purpose. In 1879 the Orient Line's main competitor to Australia, the Peninsular & Oriental Steam Navigation Company, announced their intention to commence a fortnightly service. The decision was taken by Orient Line to meet this competition, by providing a sailing every two weeks. To achieve this four further vessels were charted from PSNC, these ships being managed by Andersons & Green under the customary brokerage terms. PSNC retained any profits.

The same year, the first new steam vessel for the company was built by John Elder, the ORIENT (1879/5,386 grt) followed by the AUSTRAL (1881/5,524 grt) in 1881.

Large "well & tree" meat plate for the "Orient Line of Clipper Ships to Australia" Circa 1866.

In 1883 a mail subsidy was obtained from the New South Wales Government which stipulated that the sailings must be direct to Melbourne via the Suez Canal. This necessitated that the company set up a coaling station at Diego Garcia, in the Indian Ocean. A later mail contract led to a close relationship developing with P&O, as it called for the two companies to be jointly responsible for bunkering etc.

Ice pail showing the monogram "OPSNCo" by Ashworth Brothers circa 1880, thought to be the first china used by the company. (china of this design has been recovered from the sea bed of Port Phillip Bay, Melbourne).

A third new vessel, the ORMUZ, joined the fleet in 1886 together with two PSNC owned vessels, the OROYA and ORIZABA. This started the practice of naming all Orient Line passenger liners with names that commenced with the letter "O". Other vessels joined the fleet, some being owned by Orient and some by PSNC and a close and harmonious relationship between the companies existed until 1906, when the Royal Mail Steam Packet (RMSP) company acquired PSNC.

The line was described as the "Orient-Pacific Line" from 1901 until 1906, when after the sale of PSNC to RMSP, the line became the "Orient-Royal Mail Line". This name lasted until 1909, the Royal Mail Steam Packet Company then withdrawing from the line also removing the four ex. PSNC liners from the Australian service, which were owned by the RMSP. The company china was then marked "Orient Line of Royal Mail Steamers".

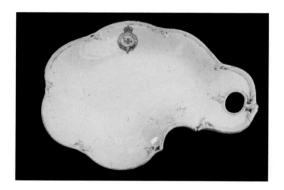 

Fruit plate showing the Orient-Pacific crest circa 1901-1906.

Dinner plate by Bridgwood & Son showing the crest of the Orient-Royal Mail Line Circa 1906-1909.

195

Crest on an "Orient Steam Navigation Company Limited" platter showing a similar "Sun burst" to one used by P&O.

Cake stand decorated in green & gold showing the crest of the "Orient Line of Royal Mail Steamers", post 1909.

Following the withdrawal of the Royal Mail Steam Packet Company, the Orient Line ordered six magnificent two funneled liners each of approximately 12,000 grt, five in 1909 and one in 1911. These vessels, the OTWAY, OSTERLEY, ORSOVA, OTRANTO and ORVIETO (all 1909) and ORAMA (1911) introduced a new standard of luxury to the Australian service, equaling if not surpassing, the liners operated by P&O.

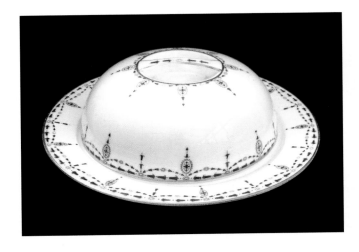 

Muffin dish by Royal Doulton "Perseus" pattern with the crest of the "Orient - Royal Mail Line" on the underside.

Large water jug by Bridgwood & Son for the Orient Line of Royal Mail Steamers.

During the 1914-1918 war all of the Orient Line vessels were involved, at one time or other, as transports or auxiliary cruisers. Four vessels, comprising a total of 45,200 grt, were lost to enemy action.

An event of great moment for the company occurred in 1919 when P&O obtained 51% of the company (acquiring the outstanding minority shareholding in 1965).

The official company crest as depicted on an egg cup circa 1925.

Logos that were used on company china prior to the Second Word War and in the 1950's.

Wedgwood manufactured several different designs for the Orient Line, including this plain white milk jug with a black handle.

Following the First World War several replacement vessels, including some ex. German liners, were obtained to fill the gap left by the vessels that had been lost, pending the arrival of a class of five new vessels that came into service between 1924 and 1929. These were also two funneled liners:- ORAMA (1924/19,777grt), ORONSAY (1925/20,001 grt), OTRANTO (1926,20,026 grt), ORFORD (1928/19,941 grt) and ORONTES (1929/20,097 grt).

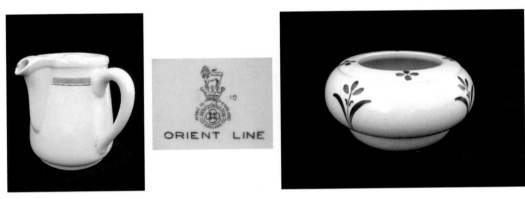

Small milk jug decorated with a brown band and black pinstripe by Royal Doulton and an ashtray bottom marked "O. S. N. C"., made by Doulton, Lambeth.

Two passenger liners were built in the 1930's, the more or less identical single funneled sisters ORION (1935/23,371 grt) and ORCADES (1937/23,456 grt). These ships broke with tradition in that they were given "corn" coloured hulls instead of black ones, the innovation of Laurence Dunn, a celebrated artist, photographer and author.

As in the earlier war, all Orient Line vessels were taken up for Government service in the 1939-45 war and the company again sustained heavy losses, the ORFORD, ORAMA, ORONSAY and ORCADES being sunk. Three replacement vessels, each of approx. 29,000 grt were built in the post war years by Vickers-Armstrong at Barrow in Furness. These, the ORCADES (1948), ORONSAY (1951) and ORSOVA (1954) were also given corn coloured hulls when built. However, the hulls were painted white in 1964 to match the livery of the P&O passenger vessels. The final passenger liner built for the Orient Line was the much larger ORIANA (1960/41,910 grt), also built by Vickers-Armstrong. Like the other post war vessels she was initially given the corn-coloured hull.

Sailings to Australia at this time were carried out jointly with similar sized P&O vessels, on a twice monthly basis, and in 1954 the ORONSAY undertook a transpacific sailing Sydney-Auckland-Suva-Honolulu-Victoria (British Columbia)-Vancouver-San Francisco. The transpacific sailings were augmented in 1958 by P&O ships under the name Orient and Pacific Line, later changed to P&O-Orient Lines in 1960. This name was dropped in 1966 and the name of Orient Line disappeared. The remaining vessels, ORCADES, ORONSAY, ORSOVA and ORIANA, became fully part of P&O the same year.

Whilst the Orient Line concentrated on the carriage of passengers (including emigrants) they also carried some cargo and owned two "cargo" vessels, the oil tanker GARONNE (1959) and the liquid gas carrier GARINDA (1977), the latter being managed by the P&O Bulk Shipping Division.

Special china was introduced for the grill-rooms on the post war liners.
Dinner plate in the "Compass Rose" pattern by Royal Doulton introduced with the ORCADES and Heart's Ease pattern by Wedgwood & Co. introduced with the ORONSAY
The Heart's Ease pattern was specially designed for the Orient Line by Edward Bawden, who also designed china for the New Zealand Shipping Company.

"Fouled Anchor" pattern made by Wedgwood introduced with the ORIANA, circa 1959. This design was by Robert Goodden.

Coffee cup and saucer from a light green dinner service manufactured by Wedgwood & Company circa 1950's & 1960's and an oyster dish by Royal Doulton, each segment decorated with flowers.

Possibly the most common of the post war china used by the Orient Line, the "Shell" pattern crockery was manufactured by Ashworth Brothers, Royal Doulton, Vitrock and Simpsons in the 1950's and 1960's. This china was made with at least ten variations of the shells.

Apart from the "liner" services to Australia and transpacific voyages, the Orient Line used vessels for popular cruises from the early years of the company until after the Second World War. The company was particularly active in cruising to Norway and the Mediterranean, in the 1930's.

Cruise brochures for 1931, 1933 and 1938.

PANAMA, NEW ZEALAND & AUSTRALIAN ROYAL MAIL CO.

The Panama, New Zealand and Australian Royal Mail Company was a brave attempt to provide a monthly steamship service across the Pacific Ocean between Wellington & Sydney & Panama. At Panama the passengers proceeded overland to the Atlantic Ocean side of the isthmus, where they joined a vessel operated by the Royal Mail Steam Packet Company, for the onward voyage to the United Kingdom.

Large ironstone platter manufactured by Bodley & Co., Burslem circa 1866.

The proprietor of the company was the Inter Colonial Steam Packet Company, which already operated services between Australia & New Zealand. The first vessels employed on the Trans Pacific service were the KAIKOURA (1865/1,500 grt), which sailed from Sydney on the 15th. June 1866, built by the Millwall Graving Dock Company and the RAKAIA (1865/1,456 grt), built by Randolph & Elder of Glasgow. The latter vessel sailed from Panama on the 24th.June 1866.

Other vessels employed on the service were the MATAURA, also built by the Millwall Ship and Graving Dock Company in 1866 and the RUAHINE built in 1865 by Messrs. J W Dudgeon, Millwall. In addition the steamer PRINCE ALFRED was held in reserve at Panama.

Unfortunately problems were experienced in arranging adequate coal supplies for the long 6,500 miles route across the Pacific and the service turned out to be less than successful, due to lack of trade. The company went into voluntary liquidation in April 1869, three of the vessels having already been mortgaged to the Royal Mail Steam Packet Company.

PORT LINE
(COMMONWEALTH & DOMINION LINE)

The Commonwealth & Dominion Line was formed in 1914 by four companies that all had long standing trading connections with the Antipodes.

The four companies were, James P. Corry of Belfast (many of whose vessels bore the prefix of STAR OF in their names), who had shipowning connections dating to the mid part of the 19th.Century; Thomas Royden of Liverpool, another shipowning company also dating from the mid part of the 19th. Century (whose initial areas of trading had been to India and the River Plate, and many of whose vessels bore names beginning with the prefix INDRA); William Milburn & Company of Newcastle/Watts, Milburn & Company, whose fleet included many vessels carrying names beginning with the prefix PORT; and Tyser & Company of London.

At the time of the formation of the Commonwealth & Dominion Line in 1914, the four constituent companies contributed 23 vessels to the new line from part of the existing fleets of the Star Line (James P Corry) and the Indra Line of T B Royden & Co., and the fleets of the Anglo-Australasian Steam Navigation Company (William Milburn) and the fleet of Tyser & Company. In addition, two vessels not yet completed were allocated to the new company.

The crest of the Star Line Limited (James P Corry), as used on the company china.

The livery and nomenclature adopted for the "new" fleet was somewhat of a compromise and consisted of the grey hulls and white deckhouses of the Tyser Line, the red black topped funnels of the Star Line, the PORT prefix of William Milburn and Company for the names of the vessels (after 1916), and the house flag of G D Tyser & Company.

In May 1916 the Commonwealth & Dominion Line was taken over by the Cunard Steamship Company and remained part of the Cunard fleet throughout the rest of its lifetime. Whilst the company was commonly known as the "Port Line" from the early years, the name of the Commonwealth & Dominion Line was only changed to "Port Line Limited" in 1937 and for some years the line traded under the name "Cunard Line Australasian Service, Commonwealth & Dominion Line Ltd".

The Port Line fleet provided a very important link between Australia and New Zealand and the United Kingdom. As the vessels consisted of high quality, fast, and for the most part refrigerated cargo liners, the fleet was invaluable to the country in both the First and Second world wars. In all nine vessels were lost either to enemy action or through collision in the 1914-1918 conflict and very heavy losses were sustained in the Second World War.

Commonwealth & Dominion Line chamber pot – note the house flag originally used by Tyser Line and an alternative bottom mark used on a cube tea pot.

Some of the vessels carried a limited number of passengers, and for these attractive china decorated overall with cornflowers was introduced. This was manufactured by Hammersley and Company and bottom marked with initially the name Commonwealth & Dominion and later the Port Line name. Passengers were able to obtain pieces of this china and this was additionally bottom marked "Souvenir".

Cube pattern tea pot for the Commonwealth & Dominion Line by Hammersley & Co .and the Port Line bottom mark. Whilst both the Commonwealth & Dominion Line and Port Line china was decorated with cornflowers, the depiction of the flowers varied slightly between the two companies.

One of the Port Line vessels, the PORT CHALMERS, took part in Operation "Pedestal", a fast convoy to relieve the long suffering people of Malta. This was a heavily defended convoy, however, out of fifteen merchant ships involved only five vessels arrived at Malta and of these the PORT CHALMERS was the only vessel to arrive without damage. A table setting in the cornflower pattern was removed from the vessel to commemorate the convoy and is still on display in the Malta Museum.

Following the Second world war the fleet was re built with new vessels of a very high standard. These included the PORT BRISBANE (1949/11,942 grt) and her sister PORT AUCKLAND, which introduced streamlining into the fleet. These were "classic" cargo liners and much admired for their design.

Apart from regular cargo services to Australia & New Zealand, during the course of the sixty-four years or so history of the company, the Port Line was concerned in a number of joint ventures with other leading cargo liner companies. An example was the Montreal, Australia and New Zealand Line (the M.A.N.Z line), which operated between 1936 and 1971.This line was a joint venture with Ellerman & Bucknall and the New Zealand Shipping Company and provided services between Australia & New Zealand and Montreal, the Great Lakes and East Coast of North American ports, via the Panama Canal. The house flag adopted provided a link with the founding companies of the Commonwealth & Dominion Line, as it consisted of the Indra Line house flag of T. B. Royden, defaced by a single maple leaf in the centre.

Coffee cup clearly showing the crest used on Port Line china (manufactured by Enoch Wedgwood (Tunstall) Ltd. & Furnivals Ltd).

The Crusader Shipping Company Ltd was formed in 1957 to provide services between New Zealand and Far Eastern ports and the Pacific coast of North America. This was a joint venture between the Port Line, Blue Star Line, Shaw, Savill & Albion and the New Zealand Shipping Company. With the approach of containerisation Associated Container Transportation (A.C.T.) was formed in 1996, Port Line being part of a consortium consisting of Blue Star Line, Ben Line, Harrison Line (Charente S.S Co.) and Ellerman Lines. The relationship between Port Line and the Blue Star Line was particularly close and in an effort to reduce costs a joint management company was formed in 1968, Blue Star Port Line (Management) Ltd. In addition two joint venture companies came into being in 1968, The Atlas Line, which operated from Australian ports to Japan and the Compass Line, which operated a service between Australia and South Africa.

However, as trading patterns changed and as a result of containerisation the fleet size diminished so that by 1977 only five Port Line vessels remained. This reduced to four vessels in 1979, two of which were scrapped and two laid up in the River Fal in Cornwall. These, the PORT CAROLINE (1968/12,398 grt) and her sister PORT CHALMERS were transferred to the Brocklebank Line (another Cunard company) in 1981. They traded for two more years with Brocklebank names, MANAAR and MATRA. By 1978 the Port Line, as such, was effectively no more and a very great company remained only as a memory.

SHAW SAVILL & ALBION CO.LTD.

Shaw, Savill & Co was founded in 1858 by Robert Edward Shaw and Walter Savill, who considered there to be great potential in a regular service to New Zealand. The first sailing vessel to be chartered and loaded by Shaw, Savill was the small wooden full rigged ship CHIEFTAIN (382 tons) which sailed from Gravesend on May the 24th. 1858. She was the fore-runner of many fine sailings ships chartered by the company, until they purchased their first vessel, the COSSIPORE (1851/836 tons), in 1865. By 1866 the company owned eight vessels and dispatched sixty-eight ships to the Antipodes during the course of the year.

In the early years of Shaw, Savill, the Albion Shipping Company of Glasgow (Patrick Henderson & Co.) was one of the most prominent competitors faced by the company. The Albion Line had been established in 1834 and used their own vessels in the emigrant trade to New Zealand from about 1855. The New Zealand Shipping Company was formed in Christchurch, New Zealand in 1873, to compete with the British based companies and this soon had an effect on both the Shaw, Savill and the Albion Line.

The result of this was close collaboration between the two British companies and it eventually resulted in the formation of the Shaw Savill & Albion Company on the 1st. January 1883. Both the Shaw, Savill Line and the Albion Line operated high class sailing vessels well equipped for the carriage of cabin passengers and emigrants and were closely involved with the carriage of cargo from New Zealand. The Albion Line sailing vessel DUNEDIN (1874/1,320 grt), which was transferred to Shaw Savill & Albion in 1883, was fitted with a Bell–Coleman cold air refrigeration plant in 1882 and was the first vessel to bring frozen lamb from New Zealand to the English market. This involvement with the carriage of refrigerated cargo was to continue throughout the lifetime of Shaw Savill & Albion/the Shaw Savill Line.

 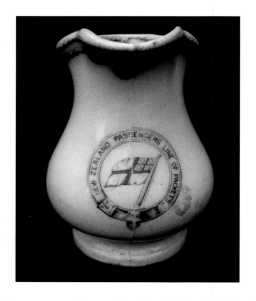

A large water jug for the Shaw, Savill "New Zealand Passengers Line of Packets" circa 1870's (Sherwin Chase collection).

Whilst chartered steamers had been dispatched in earlier years, the first powered vessels to be owned by Shaw Savill & Albion (SSA) were the single screw steamers ARAWA (1884/5,086 grt) and TAINUI (1885/5,031 grt).

In 1884 a lengthy connection was commenced with the White Star Line and a joint SSA and White Star line service was started from London, via Cape Town, to Port Chalmers, Lyttelton & Wellington using the White Star steamers COPTIC, DORIC & IONIC (each of approximately 4,500 grt). During the next few years the line developed apace and the sailing vessels were phased out. The International Mercantile Marine Company was formed in 1902 and amongst other companies took over the White Star Line, this not affecting Shaw Savill & Albion at the time, although White Star were large shareholders in the company. Later, in 1910, Sir John Ellerman purchased a large number of shares in Shaw Savill & Albion.

Soup plate supplied by C. McD Mann & Co. showing the company house flag.(this flag was very similar to the New Zealand flag which had been first used in the Colony, and liked by the Maoris, but superseded).

A cup & saucer supplied by C McD Mann & Co. showing the Shaw Savill & Albion monogram.

An event of great moment for the company took place on the 1st.January 1927 when the Royal Mail Steam Packet Company headed by Lord Kylsant, who had taken over the White Star Line and through them a large interest in SSA, announced they were now the owners of Shaw Savill & Albion. Sir John Ellerman's shareholding in SSA was acquired by Lord Kylsant the following year. This meant that the RMSP had also obtained, through SSA, control of George Thompson's Aberdeen Line. In 1928 the Australian Government's Commonwealth Line was acquired and placed under the management of George Thompson, being renamed the Aberdeen & Commonwealth Line.

Soup plate supplied by C McD Mann & Co. showing the Shaw Savill Line monogram.

All was not well with the Kylsant Empire which had serious financial problems, largely brought about by the acquisition of the Oceanic Steam Navigation Company (White Star Line), and was overstretched. This led to the collapse of the Royal Mail Steam Packet Company and its companies and to the disbandment of the group in 1933.

Shaw Savill & Albion escaped comparatively unscathed from this debacle and took over the White Star and Aberdeen Line Joint Service in conjunction with P&O, Furness Withy, the Orient Line, the New Zealand Shipping Company and the Aberdeen & Commonwealth Line. SSA were made the managers of this concern, as they were the largest shareholders.

This included the five "BAY" liners, which had been part of the Australian Government's Commonwealth Line fleet eg. JERVIS BAY (1922/14,164 grt), which became famous as an Armed Merchant Cruiser in the Second World War, when she was sunk defending a convoy.

The Furness Withy Line acquired SSA in 1933 and continued to control the company until the Furness Withy Group was itself acquired by the Hong Kong owner, C. Y. Tung in 1980.

China marked with a later "SSL" monogram, which was used from the 1930,s through to the 1960's.

Whilst Shaw Savill & Albion owned many fine liners and cargo vessels from its inception, one of the finest of the company's vessels entered service in 1939. This was the DOMINION MONARCH (1938/17,155 grt) which at the time was the largest motor liner in the world. She commenced her maiden voyage in February 1939 to Australian & New Zealand ports via Cape Town & Durban and after service as a troopship during the Second World War, she returned to her peacetime duties until she was broken up in 1962.

Attractive sugar bowl bottom marked "SSL" , a pattern of china used on the DOMINION MONARCH and a coffee cup & saucer decorated in green & gold, also bottom marked "SSL".

During the 1939-45 war one liner was converted to an Armed Merchant Cruiser (the ARAWA) and others used as troopships. A total of twelve vessels were lost and the whole fleet performed valuable services helping to keep the United Kingdom supplied with food and supplies.

Once the war was over Shaw Savill commenced to rebuild their fleet, partially to replace tonnage lost during the conflict and partially to modernise an aging fleet. The most notable vessels in this programme were four passenger and cargo liners, the sisters CORINTHIC, ATHENIC, CERAMIC & GOTHIC all of which were built in 1947/48 and of approx. 15,500 grt. The latter vessel acted as a Royal Yacht in 1953/4. Apart from these four passenger and cargo liners, many other fine refrigerated cargo ships entered the fleet in the late 1940's, such as the DORIC (1949/10,674 grt).

In 1955 the first of two liners built for a round the world service, the SOUTHERN CROSS (1955/20,204 grt) entered service. She was followed by the NORTHERN STAR in 1962 (1962/24,756 grt). These vessels differed from all other vessels in the fleet, in that they were built without cargo space and were purely passenger carriers.

Almost the final passenger vessels to enter Shaw Savill service were three "A" class liners transferred in 1968 from the Royal Mail Lines, another company in the Furness Withy Group. These were the AMAZON renamed AKAROA, ARAGON renamed ARANDA and the ARLANZA renamed ARAWA, all built in 1959/60. These vessels carried cargo as well as passengers, but only remained with Shaw Savill for a couple of years before being sold for conversion to car carriers.

In 1969 the Cairn Line was transferred into Shaw, Savill ownership and the following year the line acquired their last passenger liner, the OCEAN MONARCH (1957/25,585 grt) ex the Canadian Pacific EMPRESS OF ENGLAND. She only carried out one "line" voyage before conversion as a one-class liner, for cruising.

By this time the Furness Withy Group, like most British shipping companies was beginning to reduce its fleet, as the pattern of trade changed with the arrival of containerisation and with more people travelling by air. In 1977 a General Shipping Division was set up and Shaw Savill became responsible for the management of a number of Furness Withy Group companies, Cairn Line, Dee Navigation Co, Prince Line & Houlder Brothers. Fleet numbers continued to reduce, however, and within ten years Shaw Savill were only managing three vessels, including the DUNEDIN, a semi container vessel. (1980/18,140 grt) and the last vessel to carry Shaw, Savill colours.

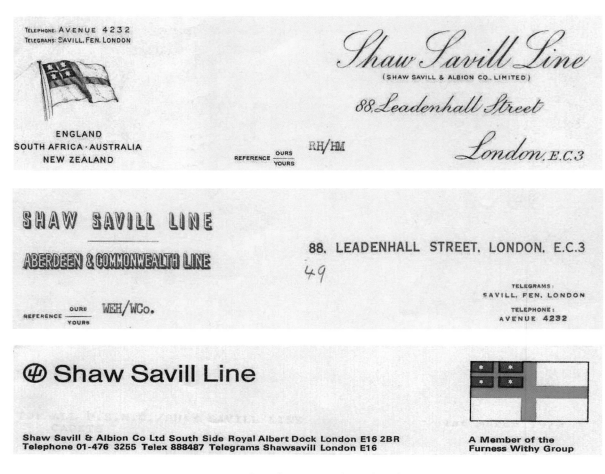

Examples of company letterheads.

209

UNION STEAM SHIP COMPANY OF NEWZEALAND LIMITED

Known as the "Southern Octopus" because of the many New Zealand shipping companies it acquired, the Union Steam Ship Company of New Zealand was one of the most well known shipping lines in the Southern Hemisphere.

The company was incorporated in July 1875, the founders being James Mills of Dunedin and other local businessmen. James Mills was already a proprietor of the Harbour Steam Company and in 1873 he had issued a prospectus hoping to attract financial support for a new company, without success. Accordingly he travelled to Great Britain in 1874, where he was more successful and also met Peter Denny of the well known shipbuilders, William Denny & Bothers of Dumbarton. Peter Denny saw the possibilities in the new venture and agreed to build two new steamers, providing 37.5% of the cost of building. This was the beginning of a close relationship between William Denny & the Union Steam Ship Company, many vessels being built at Dumbarton over the ensuing years for the New Zealand company.

Very early tureen by John Maddock & Sons Lt., Brunswick pattern.

The new steamers were named HAWEA (1875/721 grt) and TAUPO (1875/720 grt), the first of many to carry the names of New Zealand Lakes, and they joined three Harbour Steam Company vessels, MAORI, BEAUTIFUL STAR & BRUCE to provide New Zealand coastal services.

The Intercolonial passenger and cargo trade between New Zealand and Australia across the Tasman Sea was entered in 1876. The Union Line managed vessel. WAKAPITU, sailed from Port Chalmers (Dunedin) for Sydney via Wellington on the 4th. October. The Trans-Tasman services were strengthened in 1878 with the purchase of the Melbourne-New Zealand service of McMeckan, Blackwood and Co., Melbourne, together with four steamers.

The first of many notable ships built for the company, the ROTOMAHANA (1879/1727 grt) was launched at Dumbarton in 1879. A graceful vessel for the Intercolonial trade, she was the first ocean going vessel in the world to be built of mild steel and was fitted with bilge keels. She was often called the "Greyhound of the Pacific", giving forty-one years service.

Large tureen with a blue border by E. F. Bodley & Son, Longport circa 1888-1898 and dinner plate with a plain white border.

 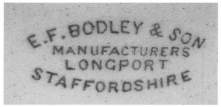

Company house flag and manufacturers mark on underside of the tureen.

The individual items of china were each decorated with different flowers – examples above.

Trade to the Pacific islands was commenced in 1881 with the purchase of the Auckland Steam Ship Company – and their small vessel, SOUTHERN CROSS (1873/282grt). This vessel ran a service from Auckland to Fiji and as the trade rapidly developed larger steamers were built for the South Sea Island services, which included vessels such as the TAVIUNI (1890/1465 grt).

Until the middle of the 1880's all the Union SS Co. vessels, irrespective of their size, had carried passengers as well as cargo; however, in 1885 two vessels without passenger accommodation arrived from the Clyde, these being the first of many cargo vessels owned by the company in its lifetime. The same year, the company took over the Black Diamond Line, Wellington, together with four steamers and a coal mine.

Large tureen manufactured by F. Winkle & Co. circa 1905.

The fleet had developed rapidly in the first ten years of the company's existence and by 1885 stood at twenty-nine steamers, with a tonnage of 30,602 tons register. Further expansion of the Union SS Co's services took place two years later, when the TEKAPO sailed from Wellington to Calcutta, India, with a shipment of horses to for use as Army remounts. She returned with jute, tea and general cargo. This trade to India continued until the early 1970's.

Chamber pot by F. Winkle & Company.

The year of 1885 saw the first involvement of the company in the Trans Pacific passenger and cargo trade when, in conjunction with Oceanic Steam Ship Company of San Francisco, a three years contract to provide regular services was obtained from the Governments of New Zealand and New South Wales. The first Union Line vessel to be employed on this service was the MARAROA that sailed from Sydney for San Francisco via Auckland on the 4th.December 1885. The company had to withdraw from this trade in 1900, after the United States annexed the Hawaiian Islands and legislation debarred foreign vessels from trading between "American ports", which included Honolulu. The traffic between Honolulu and San Francisco had been an important part of the trade for the company, as it included a U. S. Government mail subsidy.

In 1891 the Intercolonial trade was greatly expanded when the company took over the Tasmanian Steam Navigation Company, which ran services between Hobart and Sydney, Melbourne and Launceston and on the Tasmanian coast. The Union SS Co. acquired eight steamers and five coal hulks. The Union SS Co. also became interested in the mail and passenger service to Vancouver, Canada, which had been established by James Huddart in 1893. This company had experienced difficult times. The Canadian Australasian Royal Mail Line, known as the "All Red Route" (because of the red colour of British Empire countries as depicted on maps at that time) had been liquidated in 1897. Services had, however, been maintained by the New Zealand Shipping Company, who were the company's main creditors. The Union Line acquired a half share in the Canadian Australasian Royal Mail Line in 1901 and with it the management of the company, acquiring the balance of the shares in 1910. This line provided a four weekly service from Sydney to Auckland, Suva (Fiji), Honolulu and Vancouver.

In 1906, one of the most important services in the company's portfolio, the inter island route between Lyttelton in the South Island and Wellington in the North Island became daily. One of the company's many notable vessels, the triple screw turbine steamer MAORI (1907/3,399 grt) maintained a steady eleven hour schedule on the route.

During the period 1901 to 1914, fifty-four passenger and cargo vessels were acquired and by 1914 the fleet consisted of seventy-five vessels, totalling 232,147 tons. The services operated by the company were comprehensive including routes on the New Zealand coast, Inter Island, Intercolonial/Trans-Tasman, Trans-Pacific and to the South Sea Islands. As with most shipping companies, the war years were busy ones and many vessels saw active service as Troop Transports, Supply Ships, a Minelayer and Hospital Ships - and one uncompleted liner, the AOTEAROA, was requisitioned by the Admiralty and completed as the Armed Merchant Cruiser H. M. S. AVENGER. A total of eight vessels with a total tonnage of 54,841 tons were lost due to enemy action.

In November 1917 the Peninsular and Oriental Steam Navigation Company (P&O) bought all shares of the company and, whilst control of the line remained in Dunedin (later Wellington), the company was no longer New Zealand owned. P&O had also acquired the other main New Zealand line, the New Zealand Shipping Company (N. Z. S. Co.) in 1916 and in 1919 all principal offices of the two New Zealand companies were combined.

Coffee cup & saucer by Ashworth Brothers, with the P&O crest and sunburst and the crossed house flags of the Union SS Co., B. I. S. N Co., P&O and the N. Z. S. Co. circa 1918.

A major new passenger vessel, the AORANGI (17,491 grt), joined the fleet in 1924 and at the time she was the fastest motor ship in the world. She was later used on the Trans-Pacific service of the Canadian Australasian Line to Vancouver, which was set up as a joint venture between the Union SS Co. and the Canadian Pacific Railway Company in 1931 and managed by the Union SS Co.. This service was continued until 1953 when the AORANGI arrived at Sydney on her last voyage from Vancouver to Australia and New Zealand. The most notable vessel on the Trans-Tasman route was the Union SS Co's finest vessel, the magnificent AWATEA (1936/13,482 grt). She was powered by Parsons turbines and recognised as being one of the fastest liners in the world. Sadly she was sunk by German bombers in the Second World War off Bougie, Algeria, on 11th.Novemner 1942, whilst acting as a Landing Ship, Infantry.

Special china was commissioned for the AWATEA. Examples by Royal Doulton are shown above.

Further examples of AWATEA china by Royal Doulton.

The Trans-Pacific service from Sydney & Wellington to San Francisco, marketed as the Union Royal Mail Line, which had operated from 1855 until 1900 and then resumed in 1910, was terminated in 1936. This was one of many services that had been adversely affected by the generally poor trading conditions world wide. One of the two liners involved, the MAKURA, was sold to breakers. The other, however, the MAUNGANUI survived to act as a hospital ship in the 1939-1945 war.

Elegant coffee cup & saucer decorated in turquoise, blue and brown. Foley Bone china circa 1930's (E. Brain & Co. Ltd.) & H & M Williamson & Sons, Longport.

Terracotta milk jug by Lovatt, Langley Ware(c.1931-62).

As in the Great War, Union SS Company vessels were very actively involved in the 1939-1945 conflict. These ships performed services as Troop Transports/Landing Ships-Infantry, an Armed Merchant Cruiser and Hospital Ships, as well as Supply and Store Ships. A total of ten vessels were lost during the course of hostilities (59,075 tons), the most notable of these being the AWATEA and the venerable NIAGARA (1913/13,415 grt), which was sunk by a mine laid by the German Raider ORION off Whangarei, on 19th.June 1940.

After hostilities had ceased the task of replacing the vessels that had been lost was commenced and the first new vessel ordered was a new turbo-electric steamer for the Wellington-Lyttelton interisland express service, the HINEMOA. Cargo services were strengthened by the purchase of five Canadian war time built standard cargo liners and other new buildings were commissioned. As the methods of cargo handling changed and improved, more modern vessels such as the cargo vessel NGAKUTA (1962) which was fitted with electric deck cranes and the SEAWAY QUEEN (1964), a roll on-roll off, ship were introduced. The Lyttelton-Wellington express service suffered a grievous loss on the 10th.April 1968 when the steamer WAHINE (1966/8,944 grt) ran aground and foundered off the Steeple Rock at the entrance to Wellington Harbour, in heavy weather. A total of fifty-one souls lost their lives in this disaster.

In 1970, P&O announced that it had agreed, subject to New Zealand Government approval, to sell the Union SS Co. to the Australian company Thomas Nationwide Transport (T. N. T.). Accordingly in 1972 the company became jointly owned on a fifty-fifty percent basis by T.N.T and N. Z. Maritime Holdings Ltd, the latter representing New Zealand shareholders. Tasman Union Ltd. became the name of the new joint company. By now many of the Union SS Co.'s traditional trades had ceased, although some roll on-roll off services had been started. However, whilst the company returned to profitability, the Union Steam Ship Co. bore little resemblance to its former self and gradually the fleet diminished in size and considerable re-structuring took place within the group. The New Zealand proportion of the shares was gradually acquired by Brierley Investment Limited, who owned all of these by 1986. In 1996, T. N. T. was taken over by a Dutch Group and the remaining 50% of the shares owned by T. N. T. (Australia) were acquired by Brierley Investment Ltd., who then became the sole owner of the Union Shipping Group Limited, a name which had been adopted in 1980.

The most "modern" house flag design as depicted on the Union SS. Co china. This is on an egg cup circa 1960-1970 and a small cream jug manufactured for the Canadian-Australasian Royal Mail Line by H. M. Williamson & Sons, circa 1903.

Various joint venture services and companies were set up over the next few years, but by the end of the 20th. Century the last remaining traces of the great Union Steam Ship Company of New Zealand had gone forever, the final Union Shipping Group vessel being sold in 1999.

CHAPTER 7   **Cargo Liner companies**

Allan, Black & Co. (Albyn Line)

Avenue Shipping Company Limited

Bank Line

Ben Line Steamers Limited

Bolton Steam Shipping Co. Ltd.

C.T Bowring & Co. Ltd.

Buries Markes Limited

Cairn Line of Steamships

Clan Line Steamers

Common Brothers Limited (Hindustan Steam Shipping Co. Ltd)

Ellerman Lines (Bucknall, City, Hall & Papayanni)

Furness Lines (Bermuda, Red Cross Line, Prince & Houlder)

Thos. Jas. Harrison (Charente Steamship Company Ltd.)

H. Hogarth & Sons. Ltd. (Baron Line)

Hunting & Son Ltd.

Lambert Brothers Limited

Larrinaga S.S.Co. Ltd.

Lyle Shipping Co. Ltd.

Nautilus Steam Shipping Co. Ltd. (Gulf Line)

Pelton Steamship Company

Raeburn & Verel Ltd. (Monarch Steamship Co. Ltd.)

W A Souter & Co. Ltd (Sheaf Steam Shipping Co. Ltd.)

Strick Line (Frank C. Strick & Co.)

Watts, Watts & Co. Ltd (Britain Steamship Company)

ALLAN, BLACK & CO.
(ALBYN LINE LIMITED)

This was a tramp company set up by William Black & Walter B. Allan in Sunderland in 1901. The Albyn Line vessels all had names beginning "THISTLE…" and traded world-wide. Never a large company, the managers usually operated only two or three vessels at any one time. The company was bought by Chapman & Willan Limited of Newcastle, in 1966.

Detail showing house flag taken from a soup plate manufactured by M. King & Co., North Shields.

AVENUE SHIPPING COMPANY LIMITED

A British cargo liner company started by Birt, Potter & Hughes Ltd., in 1898. The company was revived in 1954 as a joint venture with the New Zealand Shipping Company and operated non-refrigerated vessels in conjunction with the NZSSCo and the Federal Line. For the most part the vessels traded between Europe and Australia/New Zealand and were named after Irish counties i.e. DONEGAL, GALWAY etc.

Coffee cup and saucer manufactured by Ashworth Brothers.

BANK LINE
(Andrew Weir & Company)

The Bank Line was established in the city of Glasgow in 1885, by Andrew Weir. The company's first vessel was the iron three masted barque WILLOWBANK (1861/882grt). She was the first of some 44 or so sailing vessels owned by the line and also the first of many ships to have a name with a BANK suffix. The first steam vessel entered the fleet in 1896, the DUNERIC (1896/1,878grt), which introduced another system of naming, the suffix ERIC. Bank Line still owned sailing vessels into the second decade of the 20th.Century and the last sailing vessel joined the fleet as late as 1912.

Egg cup with large crest manufacturer unknown & a coffee pot by Weatherby, circa 1975.

For the most part the company concentrated on the general cargo and cargo liner trades, although in 1913 they took delivery of the tanker DESABLA and owned the British Mexican Petroleum Company Ltd. from 1920 to 1930. Later they became involved with the shipment of oil from Lake Maracaibo in Venezuela and formed the Lago Shipping Company Limited (the "Mosquito" Fleet). More tankers were owned in the late 1930's, by Inver Tankers Ltd.

Double ended egg cup, manufacturer unknown and a Rosebud pattern tea pot (Royal Doulton – the same pattern of china was also used by the Union-Castle Line and Royal Mail Lines).

219

In 1933 the Bank Line took over the Bullard, King & Co. (Natal Line) service to Calcutta, Rangoon, Colombo & South Africa, which became the India – Natal Line. Three motor passenger ships were built for this line in 1934, the ISIPINGO (7,069 grt), INCHANGA (7,069grt) and INCOMATI (7,369grt).

Throughout its lifetime, the Bank Line maintained a round the world cargo service (some vessels carrying 12 passengers) and loaded general break bulk cargo in the Pacific Islands, such as copra and coffee, for ultimate discharge in Europe. This service still exists in the 21st Century with four Russian built multi purpose vessels. Bank Line, therefore, is one of the few British cargo liners companies that have survived into the 21st.Century (although this service is now owned and operated by China Navigation Company – Swire Group).

Coffee cup & saucer, manufactured by Royal Doulton.

Other examples of the markings on Bank Line china, that on the left being the underside of the Royal Doulton tea pot.

Apart from the Bank Line itself, Andrew Weir owned the United Baltic Corporation jointly with the East Asiatic Company Limited of Copenhagen and operated passenger and cargo liners services to the Baltic states from 1919 and through the U.B.C., took over the Spanish services of Robert MacAndrew & Company in 1935.

BEN LINE STEAMERS LIMITED

The Ben Line originates from the Scottish port of Leith and dates back to 1839 when the first sailing vessel, CARRARA, was bought to carry marble from Italy to Scotland. From the beginning the company was managed by the Thomson family and the names of the managers Wm. Thomson & Co. came into being in 1847. Initially the company vessels traded to Canada, however, the Far East became the main area of interest to the firm. The first steamer built for the company was the BENLEDI of 1,557 grt built of iron in 1871, by Barclay, Curle & Co. Her name was typical of the fleet, in that the majority of vessels owned by the line were named after Scottish "Bens" or mountains.

The company developed a reputation for having a fine looking fleet and sailings were advertised variously as "The Clipper Line of Steamers", or after the vessels commenced trading from London and U. K. East coast ports, "The Ben Line of London & China Clippers". Much of the maintenance was carried out by Hong Kong Chinese crews and painters were specifically carried on board the later vessels to paint the steel superstructure around the accommodation areas, in a "wood grain effect".

Tea cup & saucer by Dunn Bennett.

Detail of a china tea plate by Steelite circa 1970's clearly showing the company house flag.

Whilst Ben Line Steamers for the most part operated fast general cargo liners, some of which had high class accommodation for a small number of passengers, they also entered the container trade and in 1970 Ben Line Containers was formed jointly with Ellerman Lines (80% Ben, 20% Ellermans). The conventional cargo liner services were finally fully containerised by 1985, although the company by this time had diversified into bulk carriers, and the offshore drilling industry with jack up rigs, and self propelled drilling ships etc.

BOLTON STEAM SHIPPING CO. LTD

THE BOLTON STEAM SHIPPING CO.LTD.

DIRECTORS:
F.B.BOLTON.   C.F.B.ARTHUR.
C.H.GLOVER.   R.A.POPE.

MANAGERS FOR:
THE NORTH YORKSHIRE SHIPPING CO.LTD.

CABLES: TERSE,LONDON.
TELEGRAMS: TERSE,FEN,LONDON.
TELEPHONE: MINCING LANE 3166.

PLANTATION HOUSE,
MINCING LANE,
LONDON, E.C.3.

Frederick Bolton became a Lloyds Underwriter in 1874 and a tramp shipowner in 1885. The name of his first vessel was the RAPHAEL (1885/2,600 grt), which was named after the artist of that name. This began the custom of naming for the later vessels, all of which bore names beginning with the letter "R".

The Bolton Steam Shipping Company was formed in 1887 and further ships were built for the company over the next few years. These traded world wide e. g. from Batum, with case oil for the Far East returning with rice from Rangoon or the Black Sea run etc. and many cargoes consisted of grain or coal. The company was put into voluntary liquidation in 1917 and Sir Frederick Bolton (as he then was) retired, dying in 1920.

Cheese dish & cover manufactured by the North Staffordshire Pottery Co. for the Bolton Steam Shipping Company and a tea cup & saucer for the North Yorkshire Shipping Company manufactured circa 1964 by Ridgway Potteries Limited.

In 1921 the company was resurrected by Louis Hamilton Bolton and three second hand vessels purchased, these being renamed RUBENS, RIBERA and RUYSDAEL, these were followed by new buildings. The Second World War resulted in two vessels being lost due to enemy action and by 1945 the company had three tramps remaining. However, in 1941 Boltons had taken over the Shakespeare Shipping Company from Glover Brothers, a family closely connected to the Bolton family by friendship & marriage.

As the years progressed, the "smaller" tramp ships became less economic to operate and, following discussions with the British Iron and Steel Corporation, four ore carriers were built and the North Yorkshire Shipping Company formed to operate them in 1956. These vessels were of approximately 15,300 dwt. and were named after places in North Yorkshire, REDCAR, RIPON, RIBBLEHEAD and RIEVAULX.

The first of four bulk carriers, the RIBERA (1965/27,300 dwt) entered service in 1965, although as trading generally went into decline the shipping interests were sold to Ted Arison of America in 1982. The Bolton company were no longer shipowners, although they still continued to manage vessels.

C. T. BOWRING & Co. Ltd.

One of the oldest names in British shipping, Bowrings, was founded by Benjamin Bowring of Newfoundland in the 1830's and an office opened in Liverpool under the name of Benjamin Bowring. Initially three small sailing vessels were operated out of St. John's, Newfoundland. The trading name used in 1839 was Bowring Brothers Limited and the same year the fast sailing brig MARY JANE was purchased, she making many transatlantic voyages to Liverpool with fish & oil, returning to St. John's with a variety of cargo. The name of the Liverpool Company was changed to C. T. Bowring & Company in 1841 and at first the main interest of the firm was the slaughter of seals.

The crests of C. T. Bowring & Co., and the Bowring Steamship Company

The company developed and a large fleet of sailing vessels was operated on the Transatlantic, Indian, Brazilian, Australian and New Zealand trades in the 1860's. A regular Tyne to New York steamer service using the first Bowring deep sea steamers, TITANIA (1880/1961grt) , JULIET (1881/ 2090 grt) and ROMEO (1883/2,279grt), was operated in the 1880's and a regular coastal passenger service was set up between New, York, Halifax, Nova Scotia and St. John's , Newfoundland in 1884. This service was known as the Red Cross Line, after the red cross on the company's house flag and funnel and operated "liners" such as the ROSALIND (1911/2,390 grt) until the line was sold to Furness, Withy & Co. Ltd. in 1929.

Steamship Rosalind
Red Cross Line.

In 1888 George Bowring (a son of Charles Tricks Bowring) founded the English & American Shipping Company Ltd. This Company was set up to operate a triangular tramping service with coal from the U.K. to the Mediterranean, iron ore from Huelva in Spain to Canada & the U.S.A. and grain and general cargo from Jacksonville, Brunswick, Savannah & Charleston to the U.K.

Large water jug from the English & American Shipping Co. Ltd. circa 1888.

Whilst the company had interests at various times in sailing ships, sealers, tramps, general cargo vessels and coastal liners, one of their main areas of trading lay in the oil industry. This dated back to 1873, when the company imported petroleum in barrels for the Standard Oil Company. One of their ventures into oil was the formation of the Bear Creek Oil & Shipping Company Limited in 1890, which was managed from Liverpool, to ship oil to Europe for Standard Oil & other companies. The first of many tankers to be operated by various Bowring companies was the BEAR CREEK (1890/2,411 grt). Companies set up were the Oil Tank S.S. Co. Ltd and Bowring Petroleum Company. Ltd. Bowrings also managed the tankers owned by Lobitos Oilfields Limited. The ownership of tankers was greatly expanded from the 1930's and many of these were given names beginning with the word "REGENT", as a result of charters by the Regent Oil Company e.g REGENT LION (1937/9,551 grt).

China decorated with a green band used by the "Liverpool" company, which operated the Bowring owned oil tankers and a coffee cup & saucer used by Lobitos Oilfields Ltd., supplied by Weatherby, Hanley.

The Bowring Steamship Company Limited was formed on the 5th. April 1919 to operated what remained of a fleet of both general cargo vessels and tankers that had been greatly depleted by enemy action during the 1914-1918 war and at the same time the English & American Shipping Company went into voluntary liquidation.

Two dry cargo tramps were built to replace war losses, however, most of the fleet replacement consisted of tankers. Heavy losses were again experienced in the Second World War, seven tankers and two dry cargo vessels being sunk. Further tankers were built in post war years and one 10,000 dwt. tramp ship, the CAPE BRETON of 1940.

Sandwich plate for the Bowring Steamship Co. Ltd., by H. M. Sutherland China.

The last tanker owned by the company was the GONZALO ex. REGENT CARIBOU of 1951 (12,072 grt), which was sold in 1982 .

Seven bulk carriers were built for the dry cargo fleet in the 1960's. These were operated in either the Seabridge or Atlantic Bulk Carriers consortia. and all had been disposed of by 1982.

The final vessel to be operated by the C. T. Bowring and Company/Bowring Steamship Co. Ltd. was, however, not in commercial trade but was a research vessel capable of work in Polar regions. This was the BENJAMIN BOWRING ex. the Danish vessel KISTA DAN (originally owned by J. Lauritzen of Copenhagen). She spent three seasons in the ice on behalf of Operation Transglobe.

C. T. Bowring & Company was sold in 1980 to the American insurance brokers, Marsh & McLennan and whilst no longer ship owners, at the beginning of the 21st. Century they remain active in the insurance world, a business in which they have been involved for many years.

KISTA DAN in J. Lauritzen colours before she became the BENJAMIN BOWRING.

BURIES MARKES LIMITED

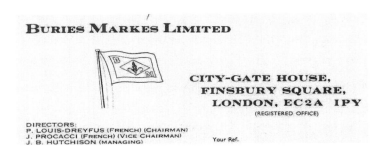

BURIES MARKES LIMITED

CITY-GATE HOUSE,
FINSBURY SQUARE,
LONDON, EC2A IPY
(REGISTERED OFFICE)

DIRECTORS:
P. LOUIS-DREYFUS (FRENCH) (CHAIRMAN)
J. PROCACCI (FRENCH) (VICE CHAIRMAN)
J. B. HUTCHISON (MANAGING)   Your Ref.

Buries Markes Limited was set up with one vessel in 1930, but due to poor trading conditions remained more or less dormant until it became the British ship owning arm of Louis Dreyfus & Co., an important Paris based firm of grain and commodity brokers, in 1938. The first vessel purchased by the "new" company was LA PAMPA a tramp ship (1938/4,238 grt) This vessel started a system of naming for the Buries Markes fleet, South American names with the prefix "LA". She survived the 1939-1945 war, whereas as two tramps delivered to the company in 1940 were lost to enemy action. An important vessel, LA CORDILLERA (1947/6,330 grt), entered service in 1947 and she was unusual for a tramp as she had high class accommodation for twelve passengers and also an all female catering staff (ex. Wrens).

Further vessels were built or acquired second hand over the next few years, none of these having passenger accommodation, although they were very superior "tramps" with excellent crew accommodation. The first large bulk carrier to be owned by Buries Markes was the LA CHACRA (1963/16,599 grt) and in 1969 the company, together with the German company J. Ludwig Mowinckels Rederi A/S and the Norwegian company K. G. Jebsen Shipsrederi A/S formed the Gearbulk Ltd. consortium to operate large bulk carriers suitable for charter. Apart from tramps and bulk carriers Buries Markes owned and operated coastal and chemical tankers, a large OBO, the LA LOMA (1972/129,961 grt) - the largest vessel owned by the company, and the liquid gas carrier NORMAN LADY.

Side plate for Buries Markes and coffee cup by C. P. Paris for the "parent" company Louis Dreyfus. The Louis Dreyfus vessels had the suffix "L. D." after their names and the house flags of Buries Markes and Louis Dreyfus were identical, apart from the letters in the corners of the flags.

The last bulk carriers built for Buries Markes were registered under the ownership of the Flower Line Limited and Baxter Shipping Limited, but they were managed by the company and ship management is now the main part of the company's business.

CAIRN LINE OF STEAMSHIPS

The Cairn Line commenced ship owning in 1883, being managed by Cairns & Young - later Cairns, Young & Noble and from 1903 Cairns, Noble & Company. The Cairn Line of Steamships was formed about 1892 and at first the company traded to the Baltic, Mediterranean and West Africa. Entry to the Canadian trade, which later formed the main interest of the line, commenced in 1908 following the take over of the even earlier company the Thomson Line of Dundee. The latter company was founded by Captain William Thomson, who died at sea in 1829. The Thomson Line was the first to carry livestock from Montreal to Leith and the Tyne.

Coffee cup manufactured by Maling, Newcastle upon Tyne. Note that the Thomson Line precedes the Cairn Line name on the crest. On the tea cup & saucer by Dunn, Bennett & Company the line name is shown as the "Cairn Thomson Line".

The company operated general cargo and refrigerated vessels with limited accommodation for passengers and the names of the Cairn Line of Steamers vessels mostly began with the prefix of CAIRN e.g. CAIRNMONA (1918, 4666 grt).

Cairn, Noble & Company were taken over by the Furness Withy group in 1928, although the Cairn Line of Steamers was not wholly owned by Furness Withy until 1967. Containerisation of the North Atlantic trades effectively marked the end of the traditional Cairn Line vessels and in 1969 the company was placed under the control of Shaw, Savill & Albion. However, small bulk carriers were given traditional "Cairn" names e.g. CAIRNRANGER (1971, 1598 grt).

Thomson & Cairn Lines egg cup.

CLAN LINE STEAMERS LIMITED

Cayzer, Irvine & Company were formed in 1878, being a partnership between Charles Cayzer, who had previously worked for the British India Steam Navigation Company, and Captain Alexander Irvine, an ex. British India Master. The Clan Line of Steamers Limited was incorporated in 1890 and the first "Clan" steamer owned by the company was the CLAN ALPINE (1878/2,112 grt), built by Alex. Stephens & Sons, Glasgow. The naming of vessels after Scottish Clans continued throughout the history of the line, until the last Clan Line cargo vessel, the CLAN MCGREGOR, was disposed of in 1981.

Initially the main trading area of the company was the Indian sub-continent and the funnel markings of the company consisted of two red bands on a black funnel, in much the same way as British India whose funnels were also black, but with two white bands. However, South & East Africa also became an important area of trade for the company.

China dish by Royal Doulton, showing the earlier crest use on the china.

In the main Clan Line operated traditional cargo liners carrying general cargo outwards and local products homeward such as gunnies, jute, tea and sisal etc. Many of the vessels were provided with comfortable accommodation for up to twelve passengers, with British Officers & lascar crews. The company also developed a reputation for carrying heavy "lifts" e. g. boilers, railway trains & carriages etc. as deck cargo. Some of the later ships had partially or totally refrigerated holds for the carriage of fruit, notably from South Africa.

The assets of the Scottish Shire Line Ltd., were taken over in 1918, which gave the company access to the refrigerated meat trade from Australia & New Zealand and led to several vessels bearing Scottish "Shire" names, rather than "Clan" names. Later the same year the British & South American Steam Navigation Company / Houston Line and its trades to South America was acquired.

Apart from general cargo vessels, Cayzer, Irvine also owned tankers under the name of the Scottish Tanker company and after talks in 1955 merged with one of the best known British Liner companies, the Union-Castle Mail Steamship Company (which operated scheduled liner services to South Africa). The result of this merger was the British & Commonwealth Shipping Co. Ltd., which came into being in 1956. This company managed the fleets of Union-Castle, Clan Line, Houston Line (whose ships had names beginning with the letter "H", e. g. HESPERIDES), and Bullard & King / Natal Line and the King Line, both latter companies being part of the Union-Castle group.

The house flag of the British & Commonwealth Shipping Company Ltd. was a combination of the house flags of Union-Castle and Clan Line Steamers, although for the most part the companies operated as separate units, this in particular applying to the passenger liners of Union-Castle.

Four refrigerated Clan Line vessels, CLAN RAMSAY, CLAN RANALD, CLAN ROBERTSON and CLAN ROSS were built by the Greenock Dockyard Company (a Clan Line company) in 1965 (each 10,540 grt .approx.). These were "transferred" to Union-Castle and re-named WINCHESTER CASTLE, DOVER

CASTLE, BALMORAL CASTLE and KINPURNIE CASTLE and were later entered into the Universal Reefer Consortium, a joint venture with the South African company, Safmarine. Subsequently the CASTLE part of their names was changed to "UNIVERSAL" i. e. WINCHESTER UNIVERSAL etc.

Later china used in the 1960's, manufactured by Ashworth Brothers ("Real Ironstone China"),

The last vessel to be built for Clan Line Steamers coincidently bore the same name as the first. This was the CLAN ALPINE of (1966-1967/8,713 grt) which was completed by Scotts Shipbuilding & Engineering Company.

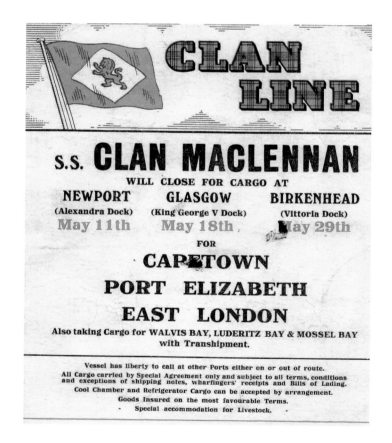

COMMON BROTHERS LIMITED
(HINDUSTAN STEAM SHIPPING CO. LTD.)

Common Brothers Limited

THE COMMON BROTHERS GROUP
Ship Owning   Shipbroking   Ship Management   Marine Consultancy
Registered Office
Exchange Buildings   Quayside   Newcastle upon Tyne NE1 3AB
Telephone: 26011 Newcastle   Telex 53267   Telegrams: "Common" Newcastle   Code Lombard
Registration 39370/England

The Hindustan Steam Shipping Company was founded in Sunderland in 1893, by Capt. Squance and Francis. J. Common, to operate tramp ships. The first vessel owned by the fledgling company was the HINDUSTAN (1892/2,420 grt) and many vessels owned by the company in later years bore names with the suffix "STAN".

In 1903 Capt. Squance retired and Francis Common died, the management of the company being carried on by his eldest son, Francis Walford Common. He was joined by two brothers in 1906 and the company moved to Newcastle upon Tyne, where the partnership of Common Brothers was set up in 1907.

The ships traded as and where required, however, as with many similar owners the Black Sea grain trade to the Ukraine was the main area of trade for the company prior to 1914. The Home Shipping Company was set up in 1913 to operate a smaller vessel, the TYNEHOLME. She was sold in 1916.

Tea pot - Vitreous Ironstone by Dunn Bennett and house flag detail.

Out of a total of five vessels, three were lost during the First World War and two sold and by the termination of hostilities the company needed to acquire new vessels. This included larger vessels more suitable for the Canadian grain trade. Accordingly eight tramps were purchased in 1918/19. Three further tramps and a tanker, the MALISTAN (1924/8,387 dwt) joined the fleet in 1923/4.

The Northumbrian Shipping Company Ltd. was formed in 1924 and at the start of the great slump in 1930 Common Brothers owned some twenty tramp ships, many of these having to be laid up or sold. By 1939 the Hindustan Steam Shipping Co. had eight tramps and two tankers, the Northumbrian Shipping Co. two tramps and the Home Shipping Company, one. During the war ten vessels were lost to enemy action and a further five were marine casualties. Four vessels were built during the war.

Whilst the company had previously owned tankers a major new venture was undertaken in 1952, together with the British Tanker Co. Ltd and Jardine, Matheson & Co. The three companies formed the Lowland Tanker Company to operate ten tankers. The majority of shares were held by British Petroleum , with Common Brothers and Jardine, Matheson each having 25%. Manning and management was the responsibility of Common Brothers. These tankers were all given names beginning with "BORDER".

The crest of the Lowland Tanker Company as depicted on the company china. Note the pennant showing the colours of the Common Brothers house flag.

Another joint company, the Vallum Shipping Co., was set up with Jardine, Matheson in 1957 to operated ore carriers on a ten year charter to the British Iron & Steel Corporation, these vessels were given names commencing with the word "IRON".

Efforts were made by Common Brothers to make their business more viable and the company diversified in the late 1950's and early 1960's. These new ventures included a management contract for the tankers of the newly formed Kuwait Oil Tanker Co and the purchase of the three tramps of the Hopemount Shipping Co. The company also operated newsprint carriers and through their subsidiary, the Northumbrian Shipping Co., purchased the Bahama Cruise Line, and with that company, the charter of the cruise liner VERA CRUZ 1.

These and a number of other ventures were not as profitable as had been hoped and in 1981 57% of the Common Brothers shares was acquired by a Norwegian businessman, Kristian Siem and his company, Norex Ltd., who were involved in the offshore industry. The last member of the Common family, Sandy Common, resigned in 1986, although the Common name still exists within the Norex Group.

AFGHANISTAN (1918/5516 grt) (World Ship Society Photo Library).

ELLERMAN LINES
Ellerman & Papayanni Lines
Ellerman's City Line
Ellerman's Hall Line
Ellerman & Bucknall Steamship Company Ltd.

For much of the 20th. Century one of the best known names in British shipping was that of the Ellerman Lines. John Reeves Ellerman who was born in Hull in 1862 entered the shipping industry in 1892, when following the death of Frederick Leyland, together with Christopher Furness and Henry O' Hagan he formed a new company, Frederick Leyland & Co. Ltd.

In 1900 the fleet of 20 ships owned by the West India & Pacific Steam Ship Company was purchased for the Leyland Line, whose managing director was Ellerman. In 1902 the giant conglomerate of J. Pierpoint Morgan's International Mercantile Marine Company (IMMC), bought the Leyland Line, although the Leyland Line vessels serving the Mediterranean (and Canada) were excluded from the deal. These vessels were now personally owned by Ellerman.

The Leyland Line service to the Mediterranean had been founded in 1821 by John Bibby (a Liverpool ship owner) who inaugurated a service of sailing ships between Liverpool and the Mediterranean. The sailing vessels were followed in the early 1850's by a steamer, the ARNO, so that services to the area were well established when Ellerman became involved with the company.

Ellerman purchased the Papayanni Line and its eight ships in 1900 and the London, Liverpool & Ocean Shipping Company was formed to operate the ex Leyland and Papayanni vessels, owned by Ellerman. The City Line & Hall Line were also taken over in 1901 and of these two companies, 50% was owned by Ellerman personally and 50% by the London, Liverpool & Ocean Shipping Company. The Westcott & Laurance Line was also acquired in 1901, this firm have been founded in the 1870's and being the remains of a much earlier line, the Greek & Oriental Steam Navigation Company of 1857. Westcott & Laurance Line traded from London to the Mediterranean. Ellerman Lines Ltd. was incorporated in January 1902. The Bucknall Steamship Lines were acquired in 1908 and the Ellerman & Bucknall Steamship Company were formed in 1914.

Papayanni Line

The history of the Papayanni Line dates to the 1840's when the Papayanni Brothers entered the Mediterranean trade from Liverpool and started services to Malta, Egypt , the Levant and the Black Sea using mainly schooners. Their first steamer was the ARCADIA (1855/1,901grt). Ellerman & Papayanni & Co was formed in 1906, the vessels being Ellerman owned and managed by Papayanni. Through most of the line's history the ships were given names with the suffix "IAN", this being reminiscent of the system of naming adopted by the Leyland Line, whereas the majority of the Ellerman Lines vessels were named "CITY OF...".

An early Ellerman & Papayanni Lines postcard.

Tureen & lid circa 1900. "Key Festoon" pattern by Minton. (similar china was used by a number of leading shipping companies, the design being first registered in 1868) and a small cup.

City Line

The City Line originated in Glasgow in 1839 when George Smith & Sons, who were Glasgow merchants, acquired their first sailing ship, the CONSTELLATION, which was dispatched to Calcutta in 1840. This began a trade to the Indian Sub-continent, which remained important to Ellerman's throughout the history of the company.

The first "CITY" vessel was the sailing ship CITY OF GLASGOW (1848/509grt) and her name commenced the system of naming later adopted throughout most of the Ellerman group, with the exception of the Papayanni ships and those of the Wilson Line of Hull.

In the Glasgow General Directory for the years of 1864-1865, Geo. Smith & Sons, 208 Argyle Street, advertised sailings of both the Glasgow and Bombay Line of Packets and the Glasgow and Calcutta Line of Packets (source Glasgow University Archives).

The first steamer owned by the City Line was the CITY OF OXFORD (1870/2,319grt) whose introduction, together with the opening of the Suez Canal marked the beginning of the end for the company's sailing vessels.

Soup plate believed to be used on both of the "Packet" services.

Chamber pot manufactured for the City Line by Dunn Bennett & Co. Ltd.

Hall Line Limited

The Sun Shipping Company, later known as the Hall Line, was founded in the 1860's by Robert Alexander and Liston Young who managed the ships registered under the name of the Sun Shipping Company. Up until the opening of the Suez Canal the company employed their vessels on a worldwide basis, however, from 1875 the company concentrated more on their already existing services to Karachi and from 1876 to Bombay. The company's first steamer was the RYDAL HALL (1871/2,114grt) and the "HALL" names continued well into the 20th.Century, although "CITY" names predominated from 1908.

Ellerman's Hall Line egg cup and company logo.

Tureen & cover by Minton and a sandwich plate with royal blue & gilt edge by Booths.

Bucknall Steamship Company Limited

Henry Bucknall & Sons were large exporters of cork from Lisbon, Portugal. Like other merchants at the time they decided in the 1850's to operate their own sailing ships, with the main object of carrying their own cargoes. They commenced replacing their sailing vessels with steamers in 1868, although at this time their area of trade remained between Portugal and the United Kingdom. In 1888 they separated their merchant and shipping interests.

Cover of company brochures dated circa 1934.

In 1891 they decided to enter the shipping trade to South Africa and founded the British & Colonial Steamship Company for this purpose, commencing a service for 1st. Class passengers only in 1894. This proved to be successful and services were extended with the formation of the Bucknall Steamship Lines in 1900.

These services extended to lines operating between the Far East & Australia to England and between the U. S. A. and South & East Africa, the Mediterranean, India, the Far East, Australia & New Zealand. However, their service to South Africa was always of great importance and culminated in the introduction of four large passenger carrying vessels in 1952/4, the CITY OF PORT ELIZABETH, CITY OF EXETER, CITY OF YORK & CITY OF DURBAN (all approx. 13,360grt). These vessels carried some 100 or so 1st.Class passengers and with their Indian crews and excellent service were very popular with passengers.

Large milk jug made for the Bucknall Steamship Lines by Furnival's. The same style of house flag was used by the company after the company was absorbed into the Ellerman group , the letters "BSL" being changed to "E&B".

Anchor-Bridgwood china egg cup and platter.

Dinner plate Circa 1934.

An elegant tea service was used on the "Big Four" passenger liners to South Africa for morning and afternoon tea. This china, "Ming Rose" pattern, was NOT marked with the company or line name. The manufacturers were Foley & Coalport (illustrated on the next page).

Ellerman Line

Whilst the Papayanni, City, Hall and Bucknall elements of the companies had their own china Ellerman Lines had its own distinctive crockery, examples of which are illustrated below.

China pattern identical to one used by the Hall Line, supplied by C. Mc. D. Mann & Co.

Coffee cup & saucer manufactured by Dunn Bennett & Co., (also manufactured by Weatherby & Sampson/Bridgwood) and detail of a milk jug by Palissy Pottery Limited.

Soup plate. Plain white with line name in black. A. J. Wilkinson & Co. Ltd. (as a matter of interest the Wilkinson mark has been mistaken for the Cunard crest).

From the first decade of the 20th.C the various Ellerman Lines operated with success on the trade routes of the world, suffering heavy losses in both the First & Second World wars. In 1948 the combined fleets consisted of 95 ships with a total tonnage of 614,174grt, this included four passenger vessels, although many of the cargo liners had excellent accommodation for twelve passengers.

As with many well known companies, the decline of the British Empire - which led to the newly emerging nations having their own shipping fleets, - coupled with the increase of passengers traveling by air and the advent of modern cargo handling methods, had a very serious effect on the Ellerman Lines. An attempt to minimize this was by participation in 1966 in a joint container operation with Blue Star, Ben Line, Port Line & Thos. & .Jas. Harrison (Associated Container Transportation Limited - A. C. T.). In 1973 Ellerman City Liners was formed to operate the conventional vessels.

China used by Ellerman City Liners showing the company logo, manufactured by Sampson Bridgwood.

The decline continued, however, and in 1983 the Ellerman Lines were taken over by the Barclay brothers, who were hoteliers. Trafalgar House (the Cunard Line) bought the company in 1987 and Cunard-Ellerman was taken over by P & O Containers (P&OCL) in October 1991, although some of the general cargo trades were taken over by the Andrew Weir group (Bank Line & United Baltic Company etc.) This marked the end of the Ellerman Line.

FURNESS LINES
(and Associated companies)

Thomas & Christopher Furness became shipowners in 1878 and the latter became involved in the shipyard of Edward Withy in 1883. The names of Furness & Withy became amongst the well known in the British shipping industry and as Furness Withy & Company Ltd. the company still exists in 2006, albeit under German ownership. During the 123 years of their history the company has owned, or been involved, with many of the leading passenger and cargo ship owners of the day. Major companies such as Shaw Savill, Royal Mail Lines, Pacific Steam Navigation Company Ltd and Manchester Liners etc. are dealt with separately. Below are given examples of china used by various companies within the Furness umbrella.

FURNESS LINE

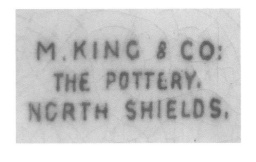

Early dinner plate manufactured by M. King & Co. The Pottery, North Shields.

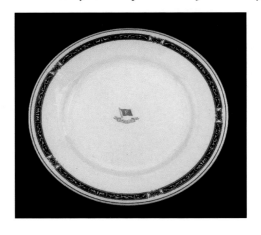

Very attractive dinner plate by John Maddock & Sons Ltd. and rim detail.

Tea pot by made by Maddock - Royal Vitreous.

Cups & saucers made by Maddock - Royal Vitreous and Vitrified Hotel Ware.

FURNESS BERMUDA LINE

The most prestigious of the many lines operated by Furness Withy was the 1st.Class only service operated from New York to Bermuda by such "glamour" vessels as the MONARCH OF BERMUDA (1931/22,424 grt) and QUEEN OF BERMUDA (1933/22,575grt). This service was much enjoyed by wealthy Americans. The china used on these vessels was generally finer than that used on most of the other lines of the group and was for the most part manufactured by Royal Doulton and Allertons Ltd .

The most well known pattern of china used by the Furness Bermuda Line, "Bird of Paradise" by Royal Doulton. The design was registered circa 1930.

Fine bone china coffee cans & saucers manufactured by Allertons Ltd.

Bone china tea plate also made by Allertons Ltd. circa 1930 and a coffee can & saucer by Royal Doulton.

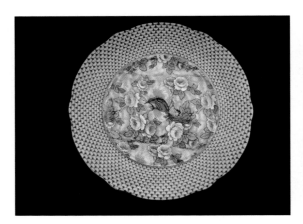

Another example of Allertons china produced for the Furness Bermuda Line, the pattern name being "Scale Border" (this china was also used by the Furness Prince Line).

FURNESS RED CROSS LINE

The Bermuda & West Indies S. S. Co. was formed in 1921 to operate services to Bermuda & the West Indies, following the purchase of the shipping interests of the Quebec Steamship Company and the Trinidad Shipping & Trading Company. In 1929 the three vessels owned by C. T. Bowring' s Red Cross Line were taken over. These were the NERISSA (1926/5583 grt), ROSALIND (1911/2390 grt) and SILVIA (1909/3589 grt).

Detail of a dinner plate used by the Furness Red Cross Line, manufactured by the American company, Scammel, Trenton, New Jersey.

FURNESS PRICE LINE

A major constituent of the group was the Prince Line of Sir James Knott purchased by Furness Withy in August 1916. This company operated a number of cargo liner services and a round the world passenger cargo service with the so-called "Compass" ships, i. e. the NORTHERN PRINCE, EASTERN PRINCE, SOUTHERN PRINCE & WESTERN PRINCE (all approx. 10,900 grt and built in 1929).

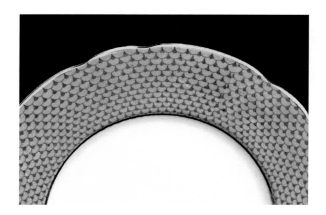

Dinner plate made by Dudson Bros. Ltd., probably used on one of the passenger vessels circa 1930.

Cereal bowl manufactured for the Furness Prince Line by Dudson Bros. Ltd.

FURNESS- HOULDER ARGENTINE LINES LTD.

An important aspect of trade for the company was that of frozen meat from South America carried in refrigerated vessels and much of this important service came to the company through the Houlder Line, in which company Furness, Withy had become major shareholders in 1906. A number of vessels were registered under the ownership of the Furness-Houlder Argentine Lines Ltd. e. g. the DUQUESA (1918/8651grt).

A double ended egg cup showing the combined house flags of the Furness-Houlder Argentine Lines Ltd.

FURNESS, WITHY & CO.LTD.

Detail from a dinner plate made by Scammel, Trenton, New Jersey & a goose egg cup.

Coffee cup & saucer by Dudson Brothers showing the last "logo" adopted by the company circa 1980.

Furness, Withy was bought by C. Y. Tung 's Orient Overseas Line of Hong Kong in 1980 and rapidly became a shadow of its former greatness. The company was re-sold to Rudolf. A. Oetker who controlled H.S.D.G., the German Hamburg-Sudamericanische Linie, in 1990 and in 1998 the company reverted to the original name of Furness, Withy & Co. Limited.

THOS. & JAS. HARRISON
(CHARENTE STEAMSHIP COMPANY LTD.)

Thos. & Jas. Harrison Ltd

MERSEY CHAMBERS
LIVERPOOL L2 8UF
051-236 5611

One of the few British cargo liner companies that continued to exist into the 21st. Century, the Charente Steamship Company, more commonly known as the Harrison Line, can trace its ancestry to 1853 when the firm of Thos. Jas. Harrison came into being. This name and the Harrison family control of the business continued throughout the history of the company. At the time of the company's beginning the main area of trade was to the Charente wine & cognac area of France and until 1865 most vessels were employed as "Brandy" boats on services from France to England. Services were also started to India and to New Orleans (for cotton) and in 1865 the company entered the fruit trade from the Mediterranean.

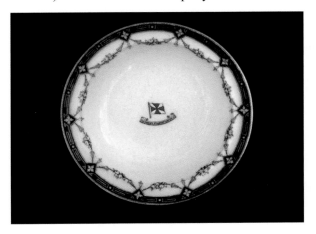

Serving bowl with full coloured house flag in the Minton "Key Festoon" pattern (identical china was also used by, amongst other companies, British & African S. N. Co.).

The Charente Steamship Company was formed in 1871, by which time the original company had regular services to India through the Suez Canal. By 1882 the fleet consisted of some 24 vessels, many of which bore the names of trades or professions, a system of naming used for the majority of vessels e. g. HISTORIAN, WARRIOR etc.

At the turn of the century Charente was operating vessels to South America, the West Indies (an important trading area for the company), the Mediterranean, India and New Orleans. A major event occurred in 1911 when Thos. & Jas. Harrison purchased the Aberdeen Direct Line of John T. Rennie, Son & Co. and their seven ships, two of which, the INANDA & INTABA were passenger ships trading to Natal, South Africa. The passenger service to Natal was maintained by the "new" company and "IN" prefix of The Aberdeen Direct Line was adopted for all the Harrison Line passenger vessels.

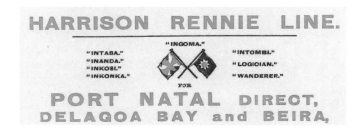

Further purchases were the twelve ships of the Saint Line (Rankin, Gilmour & Co., Liverpool) in 1917 and in 1920 the eight vessels of the Crown Line (Prentice, Service & Henderson, Glasgow, that traded form Glasgow to the West Indies. Five more vessels were also acquired in 1920 from Scrutton, Sons & Co., London, which traded from London to the West Indies.

Small sauce boat used on board the Harrison's Rennie Line service, manufactured by Furnivals Ltd., circa 1911.

Dinner plate decorated in brown and used on the passenger vessels. Manufactured by Furnivals Ltd. circa 1905-1913.

China bowl used on the passenger vessels "Norfolk" pattern Rd. No. 597783 by Royal Doulton, circa 1913.

Seven vessels from the Leyland Line of the I.M.M.C. fleet were taken over in 1933. This followed a period of great economic depression in the first years of the decade, during which time fifteen Harrison vessels were laid up and ten ships sold for scrap. These ex Leyland Line vessels were employed on the Harrison service to New Orleans and the Gulf of Mexico. Also in the 1930's the company entered into a joint service to East Africa with the Clan Line Steamers Ltd. and the Ellerman Line.

Tea pot in the most "common" design used by the company manufactured by Ashworth Brothers and Masons and a coffee cup & saucer manufactured by Royal Doulton, circa 1920.

For the most part and other than the small passenger vessels, the vessels operated by the company were traditional cargo ships, although the company was one of the first British companies to fit very heavy lift derricks to their vessels. In 1960 the ADVENTURER was fitted with a German Stulcken derrick, capable of a 180 tons lift. As cargo handling techniques evolved the company built both bulk carriers and container vessels and joined various consortia such as the CAROL service to the West Indies (Caribbean Overseas Lines).

The funnel colours consisted of a black funnel with one red band and a white band above and below the red. This led rather unkindly to seafarers referring to the company as two of fat and one of lean, after the funnel colours, i. e. an inference that the ships were bad "feeders".

Pint mug made by John Maddock and an egg cup, the latter being in the final pattern of china used by the company. NB. the name "Harrison Line" rather than "The Charente Steamship Co. Ltd.".

Thos. & Jas. Harrison withdrew from ship owning in October 2000, after the best part of 150 years. The company is now known as Charente Ltd., and deals in charts and navigational instruments. It also has a 25% interest in a LPG carrier.

H. HOGARTH & SONS. LTD
(BARON LINE)

H. HOGARTH & SONS LTD
120 ST. VINCENT STREET
GLASGOW, C.2.

The firm was founded circa 1866 by Hugh Hogarth of Ardrossan, Scotland and until 1881 the fleet consisted entirely of sailing vessels. In 1881 the company's first steamship, BARON ARDROSSAN (built 1881 by Thomas Turnbull & Son. Whitby - 1,451 grt) came into service. This vessel started a system of naming for all powered vessels, the prefix of "BARON" and suffix of the names of Scottish barons. All vessels owned by the company operated world wide, largely as "tramps" wherever cargo was on offer. The company had a reputation amongst seafarers, rightly or wrongly, as being a poor feeder ("Hungry Hogarth's" after the H. H. on the company's house flag or "Hungry Hughies" after Hugh Hogarth).

Crest used on the company china and a large water jug supplied by McSymons & Potter, Glasgow.

As the post war years passed the firm had tankers and bulk carriers built, as well as dry cargo steamers. In 1968 a major event took place when Hogarths joined with another Scottish company, the Lyle Shipping Company, Glasgow to form a joint management company, Scottish Ship Management Limited. The ships of the two companies, however, continued to sail under "Baron " or "Cape" names, the latter being the system of naming of the Lyle vessels.

In an effort to diversify Hogarths and the Lyle Shipping Company, together with other companies, formed Seaforth Maritime Limited, Aberdeen, to service and supply North Sea oil rigs. Cargoes carried by the fleet were typical for tramp ships and bulk carriers and included motor cars, bauxite, sugar, iron ore, phosphate and coal.

However, the general cargo trades went into a decline and by 1983 the size of the company fleet had reduced to a handful of vessels. The final vessel to be ordered by the company was a bulk carrier of 41,800 dwt, the BARON DUNMORE, but she was not completed for the Baron Line. The last vessel to sail for Hogarths was the BARON MURRAY (1977/20,819 grt) and she was sold in 1987, this being the end of the line.

HUNTING & SON LTD.

HUNTING & SON, LTD.
Shipowners, Managers & Brokers

DIRECTORS
C. R M. HUNTING (CHAIRMAN)
L. C. HUNTING (VICE CHAIRMAN)
SIR PERCY HUNTING
R. H. HUNTING
J. O. H. DAWSON
R. E. TREACHER
P. D. FRASER-SMITH

NORTHERN PETROLEUM AND BULK FREIGHTERS LTD. · HUNTING (EDEN) TANKERS LTD.
HUNTING STEAMSHIP CO., LTD. · FIELD TANK STEAMSHIP CO., LTD.

P. O. BOX 1 TA · MILBURN HOUSE · NEWCASTLE ON TYNE · NE99 1TA

LONDON OFFICE:- NORWICH HOUSE, 4, DUNRAVEN STREET, LONDON, W. 1.

TELEPHONE: NEWCASTLE 61017I (9 LINES) TELEGRAMS: HUNTING. NEWCASTLE-ON-TYNE, LOMBARD'S CODE.

The Hunting fleet was established in 1874 when a sailing ship, the SYLVIA, was purchased and placed under the management of Charles Samuel Hunting and W. J. Pattison, Newcastle upon Tyne. The name Hunting & Son was adopted in 1891 and from its inception the company became involved in the shipment of oil and petroleum products in bulk. However, in the early years the company also owned and operated some thirteen general cargo steamers which bore a mixture of names, such as their first steamer, the JOSEPH FERENS (1877/1,803 grt).

The first oil tanker, DUFFIELD (5,000 dwt), entered service in 1894 and most vessels/oil tankers that followed were named with the suffix "field" e. g. THAMESFIELD (1943/14,500 dwt. approx.).

Coffee cup & saucer manufactured by Dunn Bennett.

Both the house flag and funnel colours of the fleet consisted of a blue seven-pointed star over red stripes, these colours possibly being used as a result of the company's early interest in trade with the United States of America.

Whilst the operation of oil tankers comprised the main part of Hunting & Son's business the firm diversified into many other interests. These included international survey companies, aviation support services in Britain, Canada & South Africa, engineering, industrial painting, oil and ship broking, travel and freight forwarding and air chartering. The firm evolved into the "Hunting Group", although it was always very much a family run business.

LAMBERT BROTHERS LIMITED

LAMBERT BROTHERS, LIMITED.

TELEGRAMS:
INLAND: "LAMBERT, TELEX, LONDON."
FOREIGN: "LAMBERT, LONDON."

INTERNATIONAL TELEX NO: GB LN {8090-1.
                                {8170.

TELEPHONE:
AVENUE 2000.

Lambert Brothers, who were coal factors, became shipowners in 1879 with two coastal colliers, the KENLEY & MEDWAY. These and other coastal vessels were sold together with their coal business in 1896 and formed part of the well known collier company, William Cory & Son. By the turn of the century the company owned several ocean going tramps which traded on a worldwide basis, wherever cargoes were on offer. The Commercial Steamship Company was purchased from Young, Ehlers & Co. in 1905, together with four additional tramps.

At one stage of the 1914-1918 war the company was without any vessels of its own, all of these having been sunk. However, eleven vessels were managed by Lambert Brothers on behalf of the Shipping Controller. At the end of hostilities the company was without ships to manage.

Lambert Brothers took over the Temple Steamship Co Ltd. in 1926, which had been formed by Temple, Thomson & Clark a few years earlier (Lambert Brothers having had a financial interest in the company from 1923). Two years later five new steamers were built, the names of which began with the word "TEMPLE". This system of naming continued, all vessels being registered under the ownership of the Temple Steamship Co. The TEMPLE BAR (1928/4,291 grt) was typical of the fleet.

Coffee cup & saucer circa 1939 showing the company's house flag.

Over the years Lambert Brothers owned/managed a number of companies such as the Commercial Steamship Co., Dornoch Shipping Co, Glasgow, the Primrose Hill S.S. Co., the Eros S.S. Co., and of course, the Temple Steamship Co., amongst others. By 1939 the company had a fleet of ten vessels. A total of six vessels were lost in the Second World War, five due to enemy action and one was a marine casualty, being lost after striking a rock.

In 1952 Lambert Brothers managed four tramps registered under the name of the Temple Steamship Co. (TEMPLE ARCH, TEMPLE BAR, TEMPLE INN and TEMPLE YARD) and four under the Dornoch Shipping Co. Ltd (COULBRECK, COULGARVE, COULGORM & DORNOCH). The latter company was sold to Harrisons (Clyde) Ltd. in 1954.

Pint mug made by Bristol China – Pountney & Co. Ltd. Circa 1958.

Other vessels entered the fleet over the next few years and in 1968 Lambert Brothers became a subsidiary company of the Hill Samuel Group. They went on to own four bulk carriers, TEMPLE ARCH, TEMPLE BAR, TEMPLE HALL and TEMPLE HILL, which were built between 1969 and 1972. The first of the three were each of 13,500 grt. approx., and the TEMPLE HILL 14,651 grt.

These vessels were managed by Scottish Ship Management Limited and traded extensively in the area of Australia & the Pacific, including the carriage of cargoes for the British Phosphates Commissioners. All four were sold in 1977/78, this marking the demise of Lambert Brothers as shipowners, although the company still acts as ship's agents at the beginning of the 21st.century.

TEMPLE MEAD ex. COULGORM (1942/6,997 grt)   (World Ship Photo Library).

LARRINAGA S. S. Co. Ltd

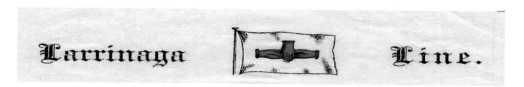

Larrinagas had a lengthy history, Captain Ramon Larrinaga owning sailings ships under the Spanish flag from 1856 and opening a branch office in Liverpool in 1862. The Suez Canal was opened in 1869 and about this time the three partners in the firm had to make the decision regarding a new vessel. Was she to be a sailing ship or a steamer?. A coin was tossed to decide the issue and it was decided to build a steamer. This decision was cemented with a hand-shake by the three partners and from thence the company house flag consisted of three clasped hands. Regular passenger and cargo services from Liverpool to the Philippines and Spanish West Indies were commenced in 1870, however, the service to the Philippines was taken over by the Spanish Royal Mail Line/Compania Trasatlantica in 1881.

Sailings with steamers from Liverpool to Porto Rico and Cuba continued on a regular basis (the former until Porto Rico was annexed by the United States) and in 1896, following the opening of the Manchester Ship Canal, a regular service was started from Manchester to Houston and Galveston. By this time the vessels were sailing under the British flag and some had limited passenger accommodation.

Milk jug manufactured by Weatherby circa 1950's. Note the clasped hands and Spanish name of the company.

A variety of names was at first used for the company's steamers, However, a pattern of naming which continued for the remaining life of the company was adopted in 1889 when the RAMON DE LARRINAGA (1889/ 3058 grt) entered service, all subsequent vessels being named after members of the Larrinaga family.

Apart from the regular services to Cuba and the Gulf ports of the United States, by the second decade of the 20th.C the company was also running regular services to the River Plate and New York. Word wide tramping, nevertheless, remained a major part of the Larrinaga operations. A total of five vessels were lost between 1914 and 1918, four due to enemy action and one was wrecked. Losses in the Second World War were even heavier when ten ships were lost. The steamers left the fleet in the 1960's, being replaced by motor ships, and the company continued to operate high quality "tramps", the last company to do so out of the port of Liverpool.

LYLE SHIPPING Co., LTD.

The Lyle family were involved in shipping as early as 1827, possibly before, although the name Lyle Shipping Co. was not adopted until 17th.April 1890. Prior to this Abram Lyle had been involved in the West Indies trade from Greenock, shipping out hogsheads and puncheons from his own cooperage business, these being filled with coal outwards and sugar and molasses, for the return voyage. He went into partnership with John Kerr in the import & export business and the acquisition of ships, and in 1865 the partners joined a larger partnership to buy the Glebe Sugar Refining Company, the family later contributing their name to the great sugar firm of Tate & Lyle.

Following the death of John Kerr in 1872, Abram Lyle took over the management of the ships and by 1873 they passed into his ownership. These first vessels were iron sailimg ships and barques and from early in the company's history the prefix of "CAPE" was adopted for the vessels names.

 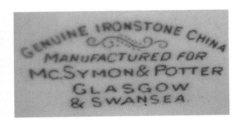

Coffee cup & saucer supplied by McSymons & Potter, Glasgow & Swansea.

The first steamship owned by the company was the CAPE CLEAR (1881/2,350 grt), this vessel being followed by three steel four masted barques. The first Lyle Shipping Company was voluntarily liquidated in 1900 and the private Lyle Shipping Company Ltd. incorporated in1903. The next steamer to join the fleet was the CAPE ANTIBES (1903/2,549 grt) in 1903, the "official" name of the owner being the Cape Antibes Steamship Company. This vessel was typical of the "tramp" steamers owned by the Lyle Shipping Co. in the years before the First World War, which traded wherever cargo was available.

Out of a fleet of five vessels, three were lost due to enemy action in the 1914-1918 war and in 1919 the directors decided to wind the company up. A new company was incorporated in 1920, the registered office having already been transferred to Glasgow in 1906. By 1922 the fleet stood at only one vessel, increasing by 1934 to some ten vessels. The number of ships when the Second World War commenced in 1939 stood at ten, being reduced to four by the cessation of hostilities – only one of these being in the fleet prior to the war.

Whilst the company vessels in the main consisted of conventional tramps, some of the fleet was of a sufficiently high standard for charter to cargo liner companies such as P. S. N. C., Port Line and New Zealand Shipping Company etc. In addition, important contracts were regularly entered into to carry phosphates for the British Phosphate Commission. In the later years the company had three ore carriers built for a 15 year charter to the British Iron and Steel Corporation. Even larger vessels were acquired starting in 1965 with a bulk carrier, CAPE RODNEY (1965/15,530 dwt), followed by six more bulk carriers built in Norway. Later bulk carriers were even larger.

In 1968 The Lyle Shipping Company joined another Scottish shipping company, H. Hogarth & Sons Ltd., (Baron Line) to form a joint management company, Scottish Ship Management Limited. The ships continued, however, to sail under their "CAPE" and "BARON" names. They also joined with other companies to form Seaforth Maritime Limited, Aberdeen, to service and supply North Sea oil rigs. The company began to experience financial difficulties in 1985 and finally went into receivership in 1987.

NAUTILUS STEAM SHIPPING Co. LTD/GULF LINE

F & W. Ritson of Sunderland owned sailing ships under their own name and steamers under the name of the Nautilus Steam Shipping Co. Ltd, which was formed in 1881. These steamers were named after branches of trees e.g. CEDAR BRANCH (1886/2,408 grt) and the company was therefore commonly known as the "Branch Line". The early vessels "tramped" worldwide, wherever cargo was on offer, however, the company became involved in monthly liner services to the west coast of South America when they placed vessels on the Gulf Line conference service. Furness Withy & Co. Ltd acquired the Gulf Line in 1903 and F & W Ritson negotiated with the new owners to keep the conference rights and continued to use the Gulf Line name.

Large water jug made by M. King, The Pottery, North Shields circa 1903.
The crossed house flags of both the Nautilus Steam Shipping Company Ltd. and the Gulf Line were shown on the company's china.

Most vessels, including a number of turret deck steamers, were operated on the Nautilus Steam Shipping Co./Gulf Line service to South America where large quantities of nitrates were loaded. However, some vessels continued "tramping" and loaded a variety of cargoes e. g. rice, timber, frozen meat and general cargo etc. A total of seven steamers were lost due to enemy action in the 1914-18 war, some being replaced by allocated vessels and prizes and by 1920 the fleet consisted of 14 ships, eleven of these being employed on the trade to South America.

The nitrate trade from South America collapsed in the 1920's and this, coupled with a world wide slump and poor trading conditions led to the end of the Nautilus Steam Shipping Company Ltd., the receivers being called in in 1931.

PELTON STEAMSHIP COMPANY LIMITED

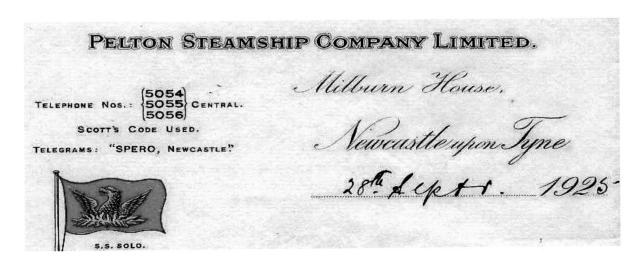

The Pelton Steamship Company Limited was registered in 1899 and managed by R. B. Fenwick and J. Reay of Newcastle, who had long been involved in the coal trade and owned the Pelton Colliery in County Durham. Their first steamer was the collier PELTON (1876/816 grt) and all their vessels were given names consisting of musical terms ending with the letter "O". Their small colliers and steamers were used in the home and intermediate trades i. e to the Baltic, near Continent, Mediterranean and the White Sea.

Egg cup for the vessel TOSTO showing the company house flag and port of registry, Newcastle.

The company survived the recession in the 1930's and both world wars, albeit with heavy losses, but in 1961 went into voluntary liquidation.

RAEBURN & VEREL Ltd.
(MONARCH STEAMSHIP CO. Ltd.)

RAEBURN & VÉREL, LTD.,
STEAMSHIP OWNERS AND BROKERS.
MONARCH STEAMSHIP CO. LTD.

The Monarch Steamship Company Ltd. was formed in 1902, although Raeburn & Verel had been together as shipowners since 1880 and at the time of the creation of the new company already owned a dozen or so tramp ships. This number included six, which were owned by single ship companies on the 64ths system.

The first vessel of the new company was the BRITISH MONARCH (1902/4076 grt) Several of the other vessels already owned by Raeburn & Verel were renamed with the "Monarch" suffix and all further acquisitions of the company bore the same system of nomenclature.

Coffee cup & saucer side marked with the Monarch Steamship Company crest.

At the commencement of the first world war the fleet consisted of ten vessels, of which six were lost during the war, five to enemy action and one due to fire in her coal bunkers. A similar high loss rate was sustained in the 1939-1945 war.

The Monarch Steamship Company operated "high" class tramps ships, which were regularly chartered to cargo liner companies, such as the Blue Star Line, although they did not change from steam to motor ships until a fourth BRITISH MONARCH (1954/5,806 grt) entered the fleet in 1954.

In 1960 the company was taken over by the Glasgow company, Harrisons (Clyde) Limited.

W A SOUTER & Co. Ltd
(The Sheaf Steam Shipping Co. Ltd)

The Sheaf Steam Shipping Co. Ltd was founded by William Alfred Souter in 1906 and the company's first vessel was the Arch deck steamer SHEAF FIELD (1906/1533 grt). The prefix "Sheaf" became the system of naming for most vessels owned by the company, after the Sheaf River which ran through Sheffield, the city in which William Souter had been brought up.

Egg cup manufactured by Dunn Bennett & Co. clearly illustrating the company house flag.

The Sheaf Steam Shipping Company operated self trimming colliers on the North East coast and deep sea tramps, some vessels being owned by the Sheaf Arrow Steamship Co., the Hebburn Steamship Co. and the Bamburgh Shipping Co. Ltd. Cargoes carried by the vessels were typical of those carried by similar tramp ship and collier owners e. g. bulk sugar, timber, soya beans etc., as well as coal.

In 1956 the company entered the iron ore trade and formed the Bamburgh Shipping Co. which was owned 51% by the Sheaf Steam Shipping Co. and 49% by the British Iron & Steel Corporation. A total of six ore carriers were ordered, four of these for the new company and two for the Sheaf Steam Shipping Company. Two of the vessels bore "Sheaf" names and four bore North Northumberland names such as LINDISFARNE. These vessels entered service between 1959 and 1961, the two Sheaf vessels being of a slightly smaller tonnage (10,867 grt) , than the Bamburgh vessels, which ranged from 11,893 grt to 13,082 grt.

In 1976, Souter's shipping interests were taken over by Ben Line of Leith and at the same time the agency, management and forwarding sections were taken over by Burmeister & Wain of Denmark. A new company was the result, Souter Hamlet Limited, who continued to manage the five remaining vessels. Three of these were Sheaf ships, which went to Ben Line in 1978/9. The two remaining were owned by Bamburgh Shipping Co, and these were sold in 1981, upon completion of charters.

STRICK LINE

As the names of Elder Dempster and the Union-Castle Mail Steamship Company were always linked with West & South and East Africa, the Strick Line was always associated with trade to the Persian / Arabian Gulf.

In October 1885 Frank C. Strick commenced operating as a ship broker and coal exporter and entered ship owning in 1887 with the NORMAND (1877/1,238grt).This vessel was only operated for a brief period, being followed in 1889 by the ALPHONSE PARRAN, which was owned by the Anglo-Algerian Steamship Co. Ltd and employed on the coal trade from South Wales to Northern France.

This vessel was sent to the Persian Gulf with coal in 1892, a venture that was so successful that Strick decided to form the Anglo-Arabian and Persian Steamship Company, this marking the company's first involvement with the Persian/Arabian Gulf. Further vessels were added to the fleet, many shareholders being domiciled in the Gulf area. These vessels were given Persian or regional place names ending with "ISTAN", a system of naming which continued throughout the lifetime of the company.

Several companies were formed by Strick's over the years including the La Commerciale Steam Navigation Co. Ltd and in 1909 the La Tunisienne Steam Navigation Co. Ltd., both with French associates (the latter to operate in the Mediterranean trade with coal cargoes). In addition joint sailings to the Gulf were carried out for many years with the Bucknall Steamship Lines, later Ellermans, and a joint company was set up together with William Cory & Sons Limited in 1928. This company, Cory & Strick (Steamers) Ltd. operated vessels in the coal and iron ore trades to the Mediterranean. On the 1st. January 1913 the Anglo-Algerian Steamship Co. Ltd. and the La Commmerciale Steam Navigation Company Ltd. were merged under the name of the Strick Line Ltd.

The fleet sustained heavy losses during the 1914 –1918 war and largely as a result of the cost of replacement tonnage and also to his advanced years, Frank Strick decided in 1919 to sell the Strick Line Ltd., to Gray, Daws & Company, who were controlled by Lord Inchcape of the P&O Steam Navigation Co. Ltd. This sale did not involve the vessels employed in the Mediterranean trades and management of the vessels on the Gulf trade remained with Strick's.

An early Strick Line egg cup.

Three new companies were formed in 1922 to operate the vessels on the Gulf trade, the Serbistan, Shahristan and Turkistan Steamship Companies, these companies being liquidated in 1928. In 1923 the Hain Steamship Company, a P&O subsidiary, purchased the whole share capital of the Strick Line, a controlling share in the Strick Line being taken over from the Hain Line by the P&O Steam Navigation Co. Ltd in 1935.

Tea pot supplied to the Strick Line by C. Mc. D. Mann & Co. (the colour of the chevrons on the house flag were actually alternate red and blue, on a white background).

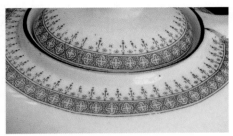

A Sutherland tea pot and detail of decoration.

When the Second World War started in 1939 the combined fleet consisted of twenty- five vessels and, as in the earlier conflict, heavy losses were sustained, some twenty owned and managed vessels being lost during the course of the war.

Circular tureen supplied to the company by C Mc. D Mann & Co., Hanley and the manufacturers detail.

The Anglo-Iranian Oil Company was nationalised by the Iranian Government in 1951,which caused some decrease in the cargoes carried by the company and in the next few years trade was further affected due to competition. Also, as the countries around the Gulf became more independent they obtained their supplies on a more world-wide basis, rather than from the United Kingdom. These changes in the pattern of trade led to a reduction in the size of the fleet to seventeen vessels by 1963. P&O formed the General Cargo Division in 1971 to operate the cargo vessels owned by the various Group companies such as Stricks, the Hain Line and New Zealand Shipping Company etc. Initially the original names of the Strick vessels were retained. However, in 1975 these were renamed in line with the nomenclature of the other General Cargo Division vessels and given names beginning with the prefix STRATH. This marked the end of the Strick Line, which from its inception had operated high class general cargo liners, some with limited passenger accommodation, between Europe and the Persian/Arabian Gulf.

WATTS, WATTS & Co. Ltd.
(Britain Steamship Co. Ltd.)

It is thought that the Watts family became involved in shipping as early as 1715, although the Britain Steamship Co. was not founded until 1884. Prior to this the firm of Watts, Milburn was started at Newcastle upon Tyne in 1856 to export coal initially in small sailing vessels, until 1869 when the first steamer was acquired.

As coal cargoes were in short supply, the company decided in 1872 to go into the colliery business to provide cargoes for their vessels and the same year the name of the firm became Watts, Ward & Co. When the Britain Steamship Company was formed in 1884 the company had three steamers and the system of naming the vessels after London suburbs was adopted, such as BRENTFORD (1884/2,143 grt). The name of Watts, Watts & Co was adopted in 1896.

Whilst the company's vessels were tramps and colliers, they were of a sufficiently high standard to obtain a contract from the British Government to transport hay from England and South America to South Africa for the British Cavalry during the South African War.

Crest used on the company china in the early years

The company prospered and by 1914 the fleet consisted of twenty vessels. However, although additional vessels were acquired during the course of the conflict Watts, Watts sustained very heavy casualties during the war. A total of fourteen vessels were lost to enemy action and a further vessel became a marine casualty.

By 1929 the fleet had risen to a total of 39 vessels, this large fleet being reduced during the years of the depression, during which many vessels were laid up, a situation common to many British ships and shipping companies at this time.

At the beginning of the Second World War in 1939 the fleet consisted of nine vessels with a further three on order and by the end of hostilities in 1945 the fleet stood at six vessels, three of which had been built during the war.

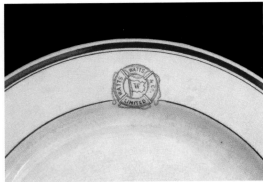

Tureen and dinner plate supplied to the company by C. Mc. D. Mann & Co., Hanley. Both red & blue decoration was used on the china.

Following the end of the war, Watts, Watts & Co. introduced a new "liner" service in 1946 between the United Kingdom and Continental ports and the east coast of Canada and a new very high class of vessels was built for this trade. The first of these was the WANSTEAD (1949/5,664 grt) built by Caledon at Dundee. She was followed by two sisters, the WENDOVER and WOODFORD.

These vessels were of a very high standard and had exceptionally good accommodation for the crew and without doubt, they, and several larger vessels that followed, were the finest "tramps" built at the time. Apart from superior accommodation the vessels were technically advanced, strengthened for ice, had knuckles at the bow and stern and steel hatch covers. The later ships were equipped with water ballast tanks at deck level to counteract rolling. These post war buildings attracted charters from well known cargo liner companies.

In the 1960's Watts, Watts & Co., apart from operating their own fleet, managed tankers and bought the Queenship Navigation Co. which had seven coasters. They also joined the Seabridge Consortium.

The Britain Steamship Company/Watts, Watts & Co. was wound up in 1968, following an offer to buy the company by the Bibby Line.

WANSTEAD 8,590 dwt, off Quebec.

United Kingdom coastal liner companies

Belfast Steamship Company (Ulster Direct Line)

Carron Line

City of Cork Steam Packet Company

City of Dublin Steam Packet Company Ltd.

City of Glasgow Steam Packet Company

Dundee and Hull Steam Packet Company

Dundee, Perth & London Shipping Company Limited

Fleetwood & Ardrossan Steam Packet Company

Hull & Leith Steam Packet Company (and the Currie Line)

London & Edinburgh Steam Packet Company

London & Edinburgh Shipping Company Limited

New Isle of Man Steam Navigation Company

BELFAST STEAMSHIP COMPANY LIMITED
(ULSTER IMPERIAL DIRECT LINE)

This company was for many years the most important line serving Northern Ireland and Liverpool, both passenger and cargo services being provided. The Belfast Steamship Company evolved from the Belfast Steam Packet Company which was formed by several Belfast merchants in 1824 and after several turbulent years the Belfast Steamship Company was registered on 25th.May 1852.

Many notable vessels were owned by the company, such as TELEGRAPH (1853) and the SEMAPHORE (1855) and later vessels adopted names ending in IC such as VOLTAIC, DYNAMIC, HEROIC, PATRIOTIC and MAGIC etc.

Many of these vessels were built by the famous Belfast shipbuilders, Harland & Wolff in the 1880/1890's. Later the prefix of ULSTER was used in the naming of both passenger and cargo vessels.

Early china used by the company and detail.

In 1929/1930 three notable vessels entered the mail service, the sisters ULSTER MONARCH (1929), ULSTER PRINCE (1929) and ULSTER QUEEN (1930), each of 3,700grt approx. The company maintained its independence until 1919, when an approach was made by Lord Pirrie of Harland & Wolff on behalf of Alfred Read's Coast Lines group to become part of Coast Lines. The latter was a member of Lord Kylsant's Royal Mail Group which included such notable companies as the White Star Line, Royal Mail, Union-Castle and Elder Dempster, a group which later collapsed and led to the prosecution of Lord Kylsant for issuing a false share prospectus.

Egg cup showing the Belfast Steamship Company crest   (also used by Coast Lines). Note the use of the English Rose, Scottish Thistle and Irish Shamrock

China used in the 1950's manufactured by Maddock.

"Hotel" China used on board circa 1960's. Supplied by Stonier & Co. Ltd., Liverpool (similar china was also used by the Trust House Forte hotel chain).

Following their entry into the Coast Lines empire, ships were interchanged between the various elements of the group and after the collapse of Kylsant group Coast Lines became fully independent financially in the 1930's. This situation continued until August 1971, when the giant P & O purchased the share capital of Coast Lines Limited and the passenger and freight vessels on the Irish Sea eventually became part of P & O Ferries.

CARRON LINE

A number of companies were involved in the coastal trade operating small passenger/cargo vessels on the routes between Scotland and England. The oldest of these was the Carron Company that was founded at Carron in Stirlingshire, Scotland in 1759 - receiving a Charter of Incorporation in 1773. At the time of its inception the company were iron founders and manufacturers of cast-iron ordnance and their most famous product was the "Carronade" Gun. Carron weapons were used by the Duke of Wellington and on board the fighting ships at the battle of Trafalgar.

The first sailings made by the Carron Company were in 1765 and were brought about by the company's need to transport their Carronades to London. However, the Carron Line as such really dated from 1872, when a local company owned by the Honourable William Elphinstone, the Carron Shipping Company was taken over.

In 1851 the Carron Line turned from sail to steam, their first power driven vessel being the CARRON. From this period in their history the line, with a few exceptions, named the vessels after rivers e. g. FORTH, AVON and THAMES etc..The tonnages of these vessels were in the range 1000 to 2000 grt and as a reminder of the company's past, these steamships carried a cannon ball just below the main truck (masthead).

Soup plate manufactured by Davenport circa 1852 for the first S.S.CARRON and the Carron Company crest.
Note the crossed "carronades" on the crest and the rope decoration on the rim of the soup plate.

The routing of the vessels was from Grangemouth on the Firth of Forth into the heart of London, where the Carron Line had its own wharves, Carron Wharf and London & Continental Wharf. Both of these were located at St. Katherine's Way in Wapping. Passenger Services were suspended in the 1920's.

CITY OF CORK STEAM PACKET COMPANY

The City of Cork Steam Packet Company originated as the St. George Steam Packet Company in 1821 and by the middle part of the 1830's their vessels traded to Bristol, London & Glasgow, as well as being involved in numerous other services across the Irish Sea. The company name was changed to Cork Steamship Company in 1843 and in 1871 the company was split into two divisions, coasting and "deep-sea".

The deep-sea division became the City of Cork Steam Packet Company and was absorbed by the Coast Lines Group in 1918. In 1936 it became a subsidiary of the British & Irish Steam Packet Company, already part of Coast Lines. The main passenger service operated in the latter part of the company's history was between Cork and Fishguard.

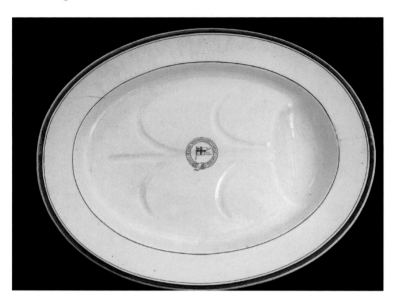 

A "well & tree" meat plate and detail of the company crest (manufacturer not known).

The British & Irish Steam Packet Company was taken over by the Irish Government in 1965 and evolved into the B + I Line, operating under the Irish tri-colour.

Sailing leaflet for the INNISFALLEN May – September 1949.

CITY OF DUBLIN STEAM PACKET COMPANY LTD.

The City of Dublin Steam Packet Company Limited was founded in Dublin in 1823 by Charles Wye Williams. The line's first steamer was the appropriately named CITY OF DUBLIN, followed by the TOWN OF LIVERPOOL. These two steamers inaugurated a service from Dublin to Liverpool on the 20th.March 1824.

Large "well & tree" meat plate dating from the very first years of the company. Buxton, Liverpool.

The company prospered and turned its attention to the Liverpool-Kingstown (now Dun Laoghaire) route, where the Post Office was running a subsidized mail service. After some opposition, the company eventually established some sailings on this route and also obtained a share in the carriage of mail. The company was incorporated in 1833. In June 1850, and after considerable negotiations, the City of Dublin Steam Packet Company commenced a contract to carry mails between Kingstown & Holyhead. Many fine vessels were used on this service, such as the ULSTER, MUNSTER, LEINSTER & CONNAUGHT. This service was to continue until 1920, when the mail contract was lost to the London & North Western Railway Company.

A magnificent soup plate decorated in green.

In 1918 Sir Alfred Read of Coast Lines Ltd. purchased a controlling interest in the City of Dublin Steam Packet Company. By this time the line was in a parlous financial state and abandoned its sailings between Dublin and Liverpool in 1919, this service being taken over by the British & Irish Steam Packet Company.

Details of a "drainer" showing the company crest. Kerr & Son, Dublin and similar details from a pint mug.

Pint mug by George Jones circa 1920 supplied by Whyte & Sons Ltd., Dublin.

The company was liquidated in 1924.

CITY OF GLASGOW STEAM PACKET COMPANY

The City of Glasgow Steam Packet Company was founded in 1831 by Mr. David MacIver to operate wooden paddle steamers between Glasgow & Liverpool. The first of these steamers was the CITY OF GLASGOW of 300 grt, which was transferred from the fleet of David Napier. The Glasgow managers of the new company were Messrs. Thomson & MacConnell, who were also ship owners and ran services to the West Highlands of Scotland. They effectively took over the company in its infancy.

The centre decoration on the platter showed a paddle vessel over a tree, with a bird on top and a fish half way up the tree (the latter being symbols of the City of Glasgow).

Messrs. Thomson & MacConnell ceased trading to Liverpool in 1850 and the vessels on this service were withdrawn the same year.

DUNDEE AND HULL STEAM PACKET COMPANY

The steamer FORFARSHIRE sailed from Hull and struck the Longstone Rock near the Farne Islands on September 6th, 1838. This disaster became one of the most famous incidents in Victorian times because of the heroism of Grace Darling and her father (a lighthouse keeper), who left the lighthouse in a rowing boat and rescued nine persons out of the sixty on board the vessel, in extreme weather conditions.

Beautifully decorated company soup plate.

Large two handled cup believed to be from the FORFARSHIRE (one handle is missing) and detail from the bowl of the cup.

Dundee and Hull Steam Packet Company mark on the underside of their china.

DUNDEE, PERTH & LONDON SHIPPING COMPANY LIMITED

The Dundee, Perth & London Shipping Company was founded in 1826 by the amalgamation of two companies, the Dundee & Perth Shipping Company, which had been established in 1798 and the Dundee & Perth Union Shipping Company of 1819. Both companies operated sailings from Dundee to London & Glasgow. Until 1834 the coastal service was conducted by sailing smacks and initially the London sailings from Dundee departed twice weekly on Tuesdays and Fridays, so as to avoid leaving on the Sabbath.

Soup plate made by Minton circa 1836. The decoration is in grey and the pattern "Lace Border" and detail from the soup plate, showing the steamer PERTH.

The company's first two steamers were built in 1834, the DUNDEE of 638 grt., and the PERTH of 635 grt., both being wooden hulled paddle steamers. These vessels commenced a theme of naming for the passenger fleet, most being named DUNDEE, PERTH or LONDON over the ensuing years.

Large charger with blue floral decoration and "portrait" of the steamer LONDON on the top rim.

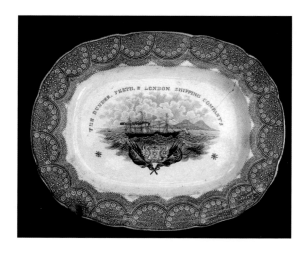

Large platter decorated in light green/grey - Minton "Lace Border" pattern - showing the steamer DUNDEE (not named on the platter).

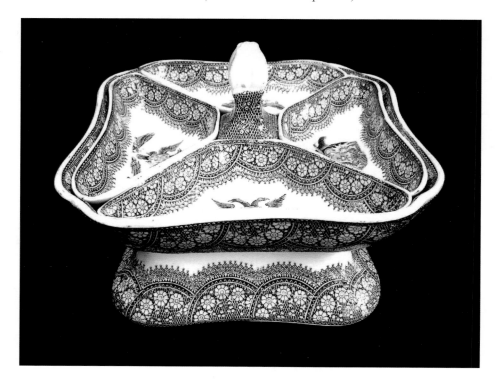

Beautiful pickle stand in the Lace Border pattern by Minton, showing the steamer DUNDEE.

Coastal passenger services continued between London & Dundee and vice versa on a twice weekly basis until the Second World War, but were not resumed in 1945. Apart from coastal services, the company also operated vessels to several other destinations and a number of deep-sea cargo vessels. They also had their own wharf on the River Thames - Dundee Wharf, Three Colt Street, Limehouse, London. The company ceased owning ships in 1967.

FLEETWOOD & ARDROSSAN STEAM PACKET COMPANY

By the middle part of the 19th.C Fleetwood had become a railhead on the route from London to Scotland and sea services were provided from Fleetwood to Scotland and Northern Ireland.

One of the companies involved in these services in 1847 was the Fleetwood & Ardrossan Steam Packet Company, which employed four iron paddle steamers on the route between England and Scotland, namely the PRINCESS ALICE, HER MAJESTY, ROYAL CONSORT and FENELLA. These vessels were all built by Tod & McGregor.

Dinner plate, depicting the paddle steamer HER MAJESTY.

(similar china was produced for the Pacific Steam Navigation Company using the same ship portrait but with the appropriate name of the vessel e. g. ECUADOR)

Egg cup in the Imari style showing the steam paddle ship ROYAL CONSORT of Ardrossan

From August 1847 until 1851 the company operated under the name of the Fleetwood & Glasgow Steam Packet Company

HULL & LEITH STEAM PACKET COMPANY

The Hull & Leith Steam Packet Company was formed in 1836, following a merger between the Hull & Leith Shipping Company (circa 1800) and the Leith & Hamburgh Shipping Company (circa 1816).

Stunning dinner plate in the Imari style, Masons Ironstone china circa 1840 and the underside of the plate, showing the Mason's mark and the line name,

After the formation of the company it initially operated coastal services between Hull and Leith and later commenced a service to Hamburg, Germany. As a result of this new service, the company name was changed to the Leith, Hull & Hamburg (h) Steam Packet Company in 1852, ("h" was added to the word Hamburg for a few years after 1852, this being the old spelling of the ancient German Hanseatic city). The company name persisted until 1940, the company then becoming the Currie Line Limited.

Pint mug showing the Currie Line Ltd., house flag & name -
Weatherby Falcon Ware circa 1960's.

LONDON AND EDINBURGH STEAM PACKET COMPANY

The London & Edinburgh Steam Packet Company was the first company to introduce steam on the route from Edinburgh to London, when the paddle steamer CITY OF EDINBURGH entered service in 1821.

A very large platter from the London & Edinburgh Steam Packet Company, bearing the coats of arms of London and Edinburgh and a "portrait" of the paddle steamer CITY OF EDINBURGH, circa 1821.

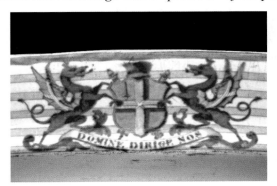 

Crests of London & Edinburgh, as depicted on the rim of the platter.

Company name shown on the underside of the platter.

The company was taken over by the General Steam Navigation Company, London in 1836.

LONDON & EDINBURGH SHIPPING COMPANY LTD.

The London & Edinburgh Shipping Company was founded in 1809 by a number of leading Edinburgh and Leith merchants, who desired to improve the service on the sea route between Leith and London. They took over the Union Company, which had been formed in 1753 to provide services from Berwick upon Tweed to London.

After the formation of the London & Edinburgh Shipping Company, sailings were initially carried out by several of the famous Leith sailing smacks. Later with the need to compete with wooden paddle steamers on the route south, two Aberdeen clippers were brought into operation in 1841. These, the NONSUCH and the RAPID were joined by a third vessel, the SWIFT, in 1843. These clippers lasted until the last one was disposed of in 1857.

Rectangular platter, depicting the steamer RAPID. She was built in 1856 and measured 524 tons. The vessel was in a collision off Yarmouth on December 13th.1857 and sank, whilst on passage from Leith to London.

Trading conditions and the need for reliability forced the company to join the ranks of the steamship owners and their first steamer, the PROMPT (1853/506 grt), was brought into service in 1853. She was followed by the EXPRESS and the RAPID in 1856.

In the 20th.Century the most well known of the company's steam driven vessels were given names beginning with the prefix "Royal", commencing with the ROYAL SCOT (1910/1726 grt). This vessel was superior in all respects to previous steamers and was built and engined by the Caledon Shipbuilding & Engineering Company. She carried approximately 100 first class and 120 second class passengers.

Ironstone china soup plate decorated with a blue/green rope border circa 1870. The manufacturer was E. F. Bodley and supplier Christie Brothers, Glasgow.

Chamber pot decorated with two thin blue lines manufactured by Bishop & Stonier, circa 1920. The crest shows the company house flag, on which is depicted the symbols of the Cities of London and Edinburgh.

Other passenger vessels at this time were the MALVINA, FINGAL and FIONA, all of these being sunk during the First World War. In 1924 a new passenger vessel, the ROYAL FUSILIER (2,187 grt), joined the fleet. She was an improvement on the ROYAL SCOT, carrying 116 passengers in first class and 130 in second.

She was followed in 1928 by a similar vessel, the ROYAL ARCHER (2,266 grt) and in 1930 by the second ROYAL SCOT. These vessels provided a thrice weekly service to and from Leith to London until the outbreak of the 1939-1945 war.

All three vessels comprising the passenger fleet in 1939 were sunk during the Second World War. Upon the cessation of hostilities passenger services were not resumed.

Like its competitor companies (Carron Line and the Dundee, Perth & London Shipping Company), the London & Edinburgh Shipping Company had its own wharf on the north side of the River Thames, Hermitage Steam Wharf, Wapping, London.

NEW ISLE OF MAN STEAM NAVIGATION COMPANY LTD.

The New Isle of Man Steam Navigation Company was founded in 1887 in direct competition with the Isle of Man Steam Packet Company and was known as the "Lancashire Line".

Ironstone dinner plate manufactured by E F Bodley & Son, Longport with an impressed date mark 4/87. The pattern name is "Seine". (identical china was also used by the Liverpool, Brazil & River Plate Steam Navigation Company – Lamport & Holt).

The company crest & house flag as depicted on the china and the manufacturer's mark showing the pattern name.

The company only owned one vessel, the LANCASHIRE WITCH (1878/311 grt), an iron steamer built by R.Steele & Co., Greenock. The end of the line came quickly and after only one year, the mortgagees foreclosed in May 1888 and the vessel was sold to Australian owners.

CHAPTER 9

Mediterranean & Short Sea Traders

Bailey & Leetham, Hull

General Steam Navigation Company (G. S. N. C.)

MacAndrews & Co. Ltd.

Mersey Steamship Co. (Morocco, Canary Islands & Madeira Line)

Moss Steamship Company Ltd., (Moss-Hutchison Line)

Wilson Line (Thos. Wilson Son & Co. Ltd.)

Yeoward Line (Canary Island Steamers)

BAILEY & LEETHAM, HULL

Bailey & Leetham was started by two sea captains, William Bailey and William Leetham circa 1854. It was known as the "Tombstone Fleet", because of the company's funnel markings consisting, of two black sections, one forward and one aft vertically, alongside a white central section.. Initially services were commenced to West Africa, but these soon ceased. The company then traded between Hull and the Baltic and London and the Mediterranean. Another important trade was carrying cotton from the United States to Revel. However, the Baltic trades became the most important and the line became the second biggest company sailing out of Hull, the largest being the Wilson Line, which took Bailey & Leetham over in 1903.

Soup plate by Brown, Westhead Moor & Co. circa 1800.

At the time of the take over Bailey & Leetham had twenty three vessels. These, for the most part, were trading from Hull to Hamburg, Antwerp & Lisbon, to the Adriatic from London and to Baltic & Russian ports, such as St. Petersburg, Koningsberg, Revel and Copenhagen etc. from Hull. There was no pattern of naming for the vessels e. g. ARGYLE (1872/1185 grt), BONA (1883/1581 grt), WILLIAM BAILEY (1883/1836 grt) and ZARA (1897/1331 grt) etc.

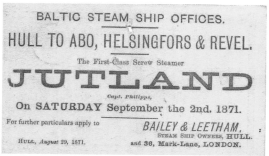

Examples of sailing notices dated 1871 for the vessels SAIDA and JUTLAND from Hull to St. Petersburg and Hull to Abo, Helsingfors and Revel.

GENERAL STEAM NAVIGATION COMPANY

The General Steam Navigation Company (GSNC) was founded in 1821 and claimed to be the oldest company in the world to operate sea-going steamships, being incorporated in 1824 as a joint stock company. At this time it was the intention to trade the company's vessels to India, North & South America, Portugal, Spain, France, Holland & Russia, however, in the event trading was restricted to the "Home Trade" limits (i. e ports lying between Hamburg & Brest) and later to the Mediterranean.

The company's first two vessels were the steam packets LORD MELVILLE (171grt) and EARL OF LIVERPOOL (168grt) which operated between London and Calais and London and Ostend respectively. In addition three new vessels were ordered upon the formation of the company and by 1825 the company possessed fifteen steamers. These were serving the near continental ports and the company was also running passenger services between London and Margate & Ramsgate. Services with "excursion" vessels remained of great importance to the GSNC, throughout its long history. In 1825 the company commenced a service bringing live cattle from the continent to London, which continued until 1891/92, and bought land at Deptford, later called "The Stowage", where a shipyard and workshops were established. A coastal passenger service from London to Granton, near Edinburgh in Scotland, was commenced in 1831.

Beautifully decorated chamber pot circa early part of the 19thC.

Large cup & saucer showing the vessel CLARENCE (760grt/1836).This vessel was operated on the service between London and Edinburgh and a similar cup & saucer shows the vessel EDINBURGH. These were manufactured in Hamburg, Germany, probably for the Masters of the vessels.

The young Queen Victoria traveled from Scotland to London on the GSNC vessel TRIDENT, in 48 hours. She described the vessel as "fine, large and very fast" and "the accommodation for us was much better than on board the ROYAL GEORGE and was beautifully fitted up". By this time over 40 vessels were in service for the company.

In 1847 part of St. Katharine's Dock, London, was leased for the General Steam Navigation Company's use and the first screw propelled vessel entered service in 1853 - the earlier vessels being paddle steamers. Initially the GSNC used a variety of names for their vessels without any particular system, however, in 1864 the first "bird" name came into use (the STORK) and most vessels from 1864 used a similar nomenclature e. g. HERON, GANNETT etc. Whilst many of the excursion vessels did not follow this system i. e QUEEN OF THE CHANNEL, ROYAL DAFFODIL and ROYAL SOVEREIGN etc. a number were named after "Eagles" e. g CRESTED EAGLE and GOLDEN EAGLE etc.

During the course of the First World War the company's vessels did yeoman service and some 23 vessels were lost. By 1920 the fleet consisted of 32 vessels and the General Steam Navigation Company was taken over that year, by the P & O Steam Navigation Company.

Detail from a white dinner plate top marked in the centre, used by the company on board their vessels in the 20th.C. Note the continuation of the use of the Globe. This was used from 1824 to signify the company's original intention to operate services world-wide. The plate was manufactured by Wedgwood & Co. and supplied by W. Huntsman, London.

Various companies were taken over by the company. These included the Moss Hutchinson Line of Liverpool in 1934, which operated services to the Mediterranean with small cargo vessels, some carrying a few passengers, and the Medway based excursion vessels of the New Medway Steam Packet Company in 1936. This was known as the Queen Line of Steamers.

Dinner plate with black border decoration supplied by C. E. Bevington to the company in its latter years, manufactured by Alfred Meakin and a coffee cup from the Queen Line (New Medway Steam Packet Company).

As with so many British shipping companies, there was a steady decline in the company's fortune in the 1960's although an attempt was made, with the backing of P & O, to enter the Cross Channel passenger and cargo trade between Southampton and Le Havre. For this purpose a joint company was set up with the French company S. A. G. A. This company, Normandy Ferries, operated the British flagged DRAGON and the French flagged LEOPARD and later a larger ferry, the EAGLE, operated a service from Southampton to Lisbon & Casablanca. These services eventually ceased, although the ferries were the forerunners of a fleet which later evolved into P & O Ferries.

The GSNC operated a variety of cargo vessels, some with limited passenger accommodation, over the course of their long history, and these varied greatly in tonnage. Typical of one type built after the Second World War was the AUK, built in 1949 by S. P. Austin of Sunderland. She was 1238grt and had a speed of 13.5 knots.

By 1971 the GSNC fleet had reduced to a handful of vessels. All of these ships were disposed of by 1979 and the General Steam Navigation Company was no more.

MacANDREWS & Co. Ltd.

MacAndrews & Co. Limited

24 - 26 Baltic Street, London EC1Y 0TB. Registered No. 147166 England
Telephone: 01-253 3456, Telex: 269783, Telegrams: MacAndrew London EC1
Also at ROYAL LIVER BUILDING PIER HEAD LIVERPOOL L3 1HF & BRANCHES IN SPAIN

William MacAndrew was a fruit importer in Liverpool and charterer of small vessels as early as 1770. He was joined in business by his sons Robert & William, the firm then becoming William MacAndrew & Sons. After the death of William in 1819 the firm became MacAndrew & Pilcher, Robert later setting up a business in London under his own name. The two companies subsequently united and their first vessel was the ACOR (315grt), which they acquired in 1857.

From the inception of Robert MacAndrews & Co, the firm traded to Spain. This close relationship with the Iberian Peninsula, including Portugal, continues through into the 21st.C. The house flag included the national colours of Spain and depicted a caravel (a small ship built in Spain & Portugal in the 15th. & 16th.C.) Many of the company's early ships were registered under the flag of Spain.

Over the years both the steamers and later motor vessels were given Spanish names, usually beginning with the letters "C", "P" or "V", e. g. the steamer CALDERON (1919/1,400grt), the company's first motor ship PINZON (1921/1,365grt) and the VARGAS (1958/2,052grt). Many of the fleet had accommodation for six or twelve passengers.

The fleet sustained very heavy losses in the 1914-1918 war and the partners decided to sell their company to the Royal Mail Steam Packet Co. (the main company in the "Kylsant Empire"). This occurred in 1917, the company then becoming MacAndrews & Co. Ltd. The same year, John Hall, Junior & Co. and their services to Lisbon & Gibraltar were taken over, followed by the Glynn Line in 1922, which had operated services to the Mediterranean for over 100 years.

Coffee cup & saucer made by John Maddock & Co. The caravel device used as the decoration on the china was widely used by the company as their logo and appeared on their house flag, as shown in the letterhead above.

After joining the R.M.S.P./Kylsant Group a large fleet renewal was carried out. However, the Kylsant Empire collapsed in the early 1930's and the many constituent lines were disposed of to a variety of new owners. MacAndrews & Co. Ltd was acquired in 1935 by Messrs. Andrew Weir & Company.

Nine vessels were lost during the Second Word War and a tenth, the FLORENTINO was sunk as a blockship at Zeebrugge.

Later MacAndrews logo used on company china (also used on glassware).

Sailings from London and Liverpool were carried out on a regular liner basis to most of the ports of Spain, to Lisbon & Gibraltar from London (Hall's Line) and to Genoa, Leghorn, Naples and other Italian & Sicilian ports from Liverpool.

Following the end of hostilities a large re-building programme was carried out and for a number of years the line carried on very much the same routes, as it had done before, The methods of cargo handling then changed with the advent of containerisation. MacAndrews and Co. Ltd, whilst still part of the Andrew Weir Group, are no longer shipowners in their own right, but charter vessels to serve the Spanish (and Portuguese) trades, with which they have been linked since the 18th.C.

MACANDREWS LINE TO SPAIN.

A company post card showing one of their small motor ships.

MERSEY STEAMSHIP COMPANY
(MOROCCO, CANARY ISLANDS AND MADEIRA LINE OF STEAMERS)

The Mersey Steamship Company was operated by Messrs. Forwood Brothers & Company of St. Mary Axe, London EC3 and ran small steamers to the coast of Morocco, the Canary Islands and Madeira at the end of the 19th.century, until 1908. The company's first streamer was the WEST. The managers from 1873 until approximately 1883 were Messrs. Forwood, Paton & Co.

Soup bowl manufactured for the Mersey Steamship Company by Brown-Westhead, Moore & Co., circa 1895-1904.

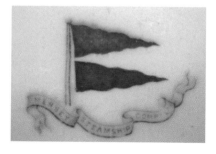

Details of the company house flag as depicted on their china and the manufacturer's mark on the underside showing the pattern name "Drayton". The supplier was Thos. F. Bennett & Co., Liverpool.

The round voyage from Wapping, London occupied twenty-five days and was popular with passengers who wanted a quiet voyage on a "friendly" vessel. In 1907 the company acquired two new vessels, the ARZILA and AGADIR. Both ships were of approx. 2,722 grt and were built by Sir James Laing at Sunderland. They each carried 72 passengers.

In 1908 the Mersey Steamship Company was bought by the Royal Mail Steam Packet Company who continued to employ the two vessels on the trade to Morocco, Madeira and the Canary Islands. They were both chartered to P. S. N. C in 1919 and sold to the Khedivial Mail Line in 1922.

MOSS STEAMSHIP COMPANY LTD., & MOSS-HUTCHISON LINE LTD.

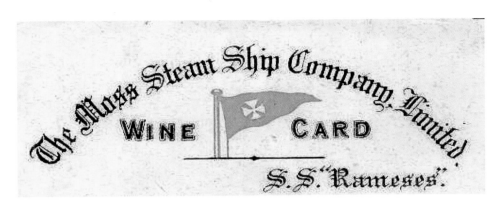

The Moss Steamship Company was founded in 1823 by James Moss, a Liverpool chandler, in conjunction with Thomas Hampson. The firm of James Moss & Co. was established in 1833 and initially the firm used sailing packets, voyaging to and from the Mediterranean ports. This situation continued until 1849/50 when the company commenced to operate a line of steamers.

In 1873, the Moss Steamship Company Limited was formed, James Moss & Co. being the managers of this firm. At the turn of the century the company maintained a weekly service between Liverpool & Bordeaux and a monthly service to Gibraltar, Malta, Syria, Smyrna and Constantinople (Istanbul). The MENEPTHAH (1905/2,808) was typical of the company's steamers at this time, which had "modern" and excellent passenger accommodation.

Coffee cup & saucer decorated with a black garland supplied by Stonier, Liverpool, showing the name & house flag of The Moss Steamship Company Limited.

In 1916 the company was taken over by the ill-fated Royal Mail Steam Packet Company, which collapsed in the early 1930's. This resulted in a new name for James Moss & Co, which became James Moss & Co. (Moss Line) Ltd.

A major development occurred in 1934 when the company merged with that of J & P Hutchison Ltd., of Glasgow which had been established in 1863 and operated services, for the most part, to French ports. The result of this merger was the creation of Moss-Hutchison Line Limited and the introduction of the letters "M" & "H" beside the Maltese Cross on the original Moss Steamship Company house flag.

 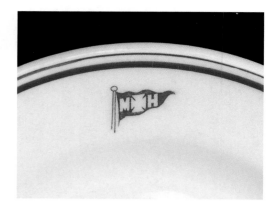

Detail from a dinner plate supplied by Stonier & Co., Liverpool, showing the Moss-Hutchison Line house flag (the actual colour of the house flag was red with a white cross and lettering) and detail of a dinner plate manufactured by Maddock & Co., circa 1960/1970.

The following year (1935) the company was taken over by the General Steam Navigation Company (GSNC) and thus became part of the giant P&O conglomerate, who already owned the GSNC.

At the beginning of the Second World War the fleet stood at 17 vessels, eight of these being lost to enemy action These were partially replaced in 1949 by second hand vessels and other ships, which were transferred from within the group. This fleet was later enhanced by four motor ships.

The P&O General Cargo Division was formed in 1971 and this marked the loss of identity of many of the constituent companies within the P&O Group, including the Moss-Hutchison Line Ltd. The last two vessels of the Moss-Hutchison Line were both motor ships and these were laid up in 1978, being sold the following year.

A company postcard of the SETI, built in 1902 by Sir Raylton Dixon & Co. Ltd, Middlesbrough.

WILSON LINE

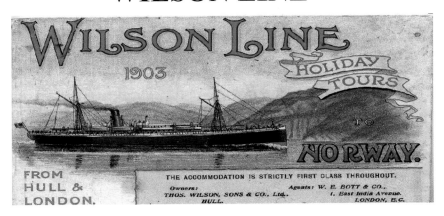

The most well known ship owner to operate out of the North East coast port of Hull, the firm of Thos. Wilson, Sons & Co. Ltd. dated from 1841 and at one time had the largest number of ships under private ownership of any shipping company. Thomas Wilson, who was already an importer of Swedish iron ore, was actively involved in ship owning from 1831, when in partnership with John Beckington, John Hudson and Thomas Hudson a small wooden schooner, the SWIFT, was acquired. This was followed by another schooner, the PETER & JANE, and a brigantine, the OSWY. Initially the company was known as Beckington, Wilson & Co. thence from 1836 as Wilson, Hudson & Co., after Beckington retired. The Hudsons left the business in 1841 and this marked the beginning of the "Wilson Line", which for many years after remained a family firm.

From the beginning, the company was closely involved with trades to Scandinavia and in particular to Sweden. In later years the line had several "deep sea" routes, notably with cargo and passengers to North America and India, the Mediterranean & the Levant. In 1840, mail subsidies were obtained from the Swedish & Norwegian Governments and, as a result, the Wilson's decided to charter three steamers from other companies, so that they could run regular services to both Norway & Sweden. This arrangement lasted until 1842 and was then suspended until 1850.

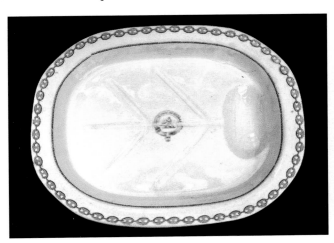

"Well & Tree" meat plate base marked Thomas Wilson Sons & Co.

The first power driven vessel owned by the Wilson Line was the paddle steamer COURIER (1850/323 grt), which was built for the Hull & Leith Steam Packet Company and bought from them in 1853. The first steamer built for Thomas Wilson, Sons & Co. was the SCANDINAVIAN (1852/423 grt.). The fleet expanded rapidly and some thirty-one vessels were acquired between 1859 and 1868, most of these having names ending in the letter "O".Apart from second hand and chartered vessels this system of nomenclature was adopted throughout the life time of the company.

Following the opening of the Suez Canal in 1869 the Wilson Line commenced trading to India with the ORLANDO, which sailed from London to Bombay in 1871. Other vessels followed and the ports called at included Madras, Calcutta and Colombo, although the service did not really settle down until the early 1880's. In 1875 the company took the major decision to enter the North Atlantic trade and the OTHELLO (which had previously employed on the service to India) sailed from Hull to New York in January. This commenced a service of great importance to the firm. By the turn of the century large volumes of cargo were carried to and from the United States, as well as passengers, via London. A joint company, the Wilsons & Furness Leyland Line, was started in 1896.

*Fruit plate decorated with a blue "anchor" chain top marked
"Thos. Wilson Sons & Co. Hull" Circa 1890.*

The local firm of Brownslow, Marsdin and Company was taken over in 1878, together with seven vessels which they had employed on regular services to Hamburg, Antwerp & Dunkirk.

*Large platter manufactured for Thomas Wilson Sons & Co. by James F. Wileman circa 1869-1892 and a
small cream jug with a gilt rim.
(The house flag was changed from a pennant to a burgee, circa 1900).*

As well as the services to the United States and India, the company's routes to Scandinavia, the Baltic and to the Mediterranean and the Adriatic were flourishing and in addition to 1st. and 2nd. Class passengers and cargo, large numbers of Swedish & Norwegian emigrants and Jewish refugees from the Baltic States were carried to Hull. Most of these traveled on to Liverpool by train, where they boarded vessels to carry them to America, some however, settled in Hull. The carriage of emigrants was lucrative until 1914 and was then suspended during the 1914-1818 war years, resuming again in 1918 until it more or less ceased in 1922. The title of the firm changed in 1891 to Thomas Wilson Sons & Co. Ltd., when it became a private limited company.

Soup plate with a blue border top marked "Wilson Line"

The year of 1903 saw a dramatic increase in the size of the fleet when the Wilson Line acquired the long established Hull firm of Bailey & Leetham, together with their twenty-three vessels. This firm was actively involved in the Baltic trade from Hull, with services to St. Petersberg, Koningsberg, Copenhagen and Revel as well as to Hamburg and from London to Venice, Trieste and Palermo. Therefore, it was somewhat of a rival to the Wilson Line. After the take over, the fleet was numerically at its high point with ninety-nine vessels and four tugs under its ownership in 1904.

Large fruit plate showing the name of the Wilson Line steamer SPERO (1896). She had accommodation for 12 1ˢᵗ.class and 203 steerage passengers when first built.

In 1906 a new joint company, the "Wilsons and North Eastern Railway Shipping Company," was set up by the Wilson Line and the North Eastern Railway Company to operate services to Hamburg, Antwerp, Ghent & Dunkirk. This company together with other Humber companies came under one management, the Associated Humber Lines (A.H.L) in 1935. A. H. L. was nationalised in 1948, when the four British Railway companies were taken over by the British Transport Commission.

At the beginning of the 1914-1918 war the Wilson Line owned eighty-four ships and suffered very grievous losses, at a time when lines from non combatant countries were able to build up their fleets and trade.

Tea plate decorated with a garland of green flowers. Bridgwood & Co., circa 1936 and a tea plate decorated in light green. The manufacturer of the latter was Cauldon & the supplier Stonier & Co., Liverpool.

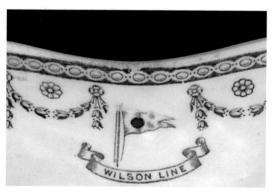

Rectangular dish made by Cauldon Ware.

This situation was of great concern to the Wilson family and in 1916 the decision was taken to sell the company to Sir John Ellerman. The name of the line was changed to Ellerman's Wilson Line Limited in January 1917, although unlike the other Ellerman owned companies the Wilson line retained its individuality and livery and was personally owned by Sir. John Ellerman. In this respect, the livery of the ships was very striking, as at a time when the hull colours of most ships was either black or grey (unlike the multitude of hull colours seen in the 21st C), the Wilson Line ships had red black topped funnels, brown derricks, white upper works and green hulls. This led to their being known as "Wilson's parrots" by the people on Humberside.

Large water jug marked with the name "Ellerman's Wilson Line Ltd."

During the course of the war the company lost forty vessels, all but four to torpedoes or mines etc. and upon cessation of hostilities new vessels were ordered to replace the losses and others bought from the Shipping Controller. The emigrant trade to the U. S. A. and Canada was resumed for a few years, until restrictions were imposed on the number of emigrants allowed and the trade collapsed in 1922.

As with most companies, the late 1920's and 1930's were difficult times for the Wilson Line, although some services were profitable, in particular cruises and round voyages to Danish & Norwegian ports. These were started in 1932 by the CALYPSO (e.x ALEXANDRA WOERMANN (1898/3,820 grt). Two Ellerman City Line passenger vessels, the CITY OF PARIS and later the CITY OF NAGPUR, were chartered between 1934 and 1939 to run weekly summer cruises from Hull to Oslo.

China with a gilt rim and the company name in brown. Aynsley China.

The Second World War proved to be just as disastrous to the company as the earlier one and, from having thirty-four vessels in 1939, the fleet was reduced to just nine by 1945. Some officers and crew had a particularly exciting war, as they were recruited to man five motor gun-boats to run supplies of essential ball bearings from neutral Sweden, through a German blockade to England.

A major rebuilding programme was commenced in 1945 and by 1952 twenty new vessels had joined the fleet, the majority of these being small and destined for the trades to Scandinavia/the Baltic and the Mediterranean/Adriatic. Almost invariably these vessels were built to a pre-war design and powered by triple expansion steam reciprocating engines, supplemented by low-pressure turbines.

Tea pot manufactured by Weatherby, Hanley circa 1970. This is the most "common" Wilson Line china.

Most vessels were provided with excellent accommodation for twelve passengers and six weeks round voyages to the Mediterranean were very popular, the mid-summer sailings being filled with school teachers during the long summer vacation. The autumn voyages were largely filled with boarding house owners from Scarborough & Blackpool, at the end of their busy holiday season.

The Indian trade was finished in 1953 and the transatlantic service to United States ports was terminated in 1961 after eighty-six years continuous trade, the services to Canada being discontinued in 1967.

Dinner plate decorated in blue.

Two vessels were built post-war with greater passenger accommodation. The first, BORODINO (1950/3,206 grt), had berths for 36 first class and 20 third class passengers and operated to Copenhagen. She carried large quantities of refrigerated produce, such as bacon and butter. The second was the SPERO (1966/6,916 grt), a ro-ro vessel with accommodation for 400 passengers. She was the Wilson Line's contribution to a consortium - the England Sweden Line. This company was set up in 1966 jointly with the Swedish companies Swedish Lloyd and Svea Line to provide a regular liner service between England and Gothenburg, Sweden (which proved to be a less than successful operation).

Dinner plate with olive green border and floral decoration - Adams ironstone china circa 1970, a small cream jug circa also 1970's with a broad green/blue band at the rim and a tea cup and saucer, probably used on the SPERO of 1966.

Attempts were made to provide a modern fleet and more efficient cargo vessels such as five vessels of the SALERNO class were built in 1965/66, followed by two ro-ro vessels with stern doors in 1969, the DESTRO & DOMINO. In 1979 the HERO, a ro-ro vessel jointly owned by the Wilson Line and the Danish company D. F. D. S., was built for service between Hull & Esbjerg, specifically to carry bacon and dairy produce.

Other new vessels were built and other joint ventures attempted in the 1970's. However, as happened to so many British companies, the fleet gradually diminished in size largely due to a combination of difficult trading conditions, over capacity and the use of cheaper "flag of convenience vessels and by 1981 the Wilson Line was no more.

YEOWARD LINE

(CANARY ISLAND STEAMERS LIMITED)

The Yeoward Brothers commenced business in Liverpool in 1894 as ship brokers & fruit merchants and from the beginning were involved in the carriage of bananas, tomatoes and potatoes from the Canary Islands.

They chartered their first vessels in 1898 and purchased their first steamer, AVOCET, from the Cork Steamship Company Limited in 1900. This steamer set both the system of nomenclature for all future vessels, which were named after Spanish birds, and the lay out of the steamers themselves - these having three masts with the engines being located three-quarters aft.

Soup plate supplied by Stonier & Co., Liverpool showing the company house flag.

More vessels with limited passenger accommodation were acquired and, as voyages on these vessels proved very popular, the first steamer with better and larger provision for passengers, the ARDEOLA, was built for the company in 1903. Three even larger steamers were built before the first world war broke out in 1914, these vessels being used for popular cruises from Liverpool to Portugal the Canary Islands and Madeira. Later, calls were made at ports in Northern Spain and Morocco and occasional cruises made to the Baltic.

Four vessels were lost during the course of the war although one new vessel, the second AGUILA (3,255 grt), was completed in 1917 and two Norwegian vessels were managed by the company on behalf of the Shipping Controller.

Three new vessels joined the fleet over the next few years, the second ALONDRA (1922), the AVOCETA (1923) and finally the second ALCA (1927). By this time the steamers were capable of carrying 120 passengers in excellent accommodation, as well as having cargo spaces for a large amount of fruit and vegetables etc.

China dinner plate decorated with violets, bottom marked with the line name and the name of the suppliers. Stonier & Co., Liverpool.

The Yeoward Line fleet was decimated during the Second World War and only the ALCA survived the conflict and, after refitting, resuming normal service in 1946,.

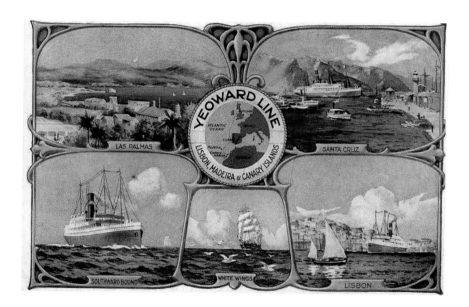

Additional vessels were provided in the post-war years by the C. Clausen Line of Copenhagen. During the fruit season two vessels were chartered for three years from Manchester Liners. However, the Yeoward Line was never the same after the war and the line was wound up in 1959.

CHAPTER 10   **Sailing Packets & Miscellaneous**

Arctic Expedition of 1875

Blackwall Line of Packets

British Antarctic Expedition of 1912 – TERRA NOVA

Devitt & Moore (Australian Line of Steam & Clipper Ships)

Great Ship Company (the GREAT EASTERN including the
Telegraph Construction & Maintenance Company)

Honourable East India Company (United Company of Merchants
of England trading to the East Indies)

Marine Service

S.S. GREAT BRITAIN (Great Western Steamship Company)

ARCTIC EXPEDITION OF 1875

The British Arctic Expedition of 1875-76 was lead by Captain George Nares, the expedition's vessels being H.M.S. ALERT and H.M.S. DISCOVERY.

China for use on the expedition was manufactured by W. T. Copeland and Sons.

The illustration on the left shows the underside of a soup plate made for H.M.S.DISCOVERY and that on the right, the manufacturer's detail. The china for the expedition was marked on the underside with the name of the appropriate vessel – ALERT or DISCOVERY.

A variation in brown (according to the National Maritime Museum, Greenwich, the crew were provided with an earthenware dinner services printed in blue, black or brown, a china service in black being used by the officers).

BLACKWALL LINE OF PACKETS
(and Money Wigram & Sons Line of Steam & Packet Ships to Australia)

Richard Green of Blackwall, London was a shipbuilder of considerable renown, building many of the great 'Blackwall Frigates' for the Honourable East India Company, at the beginning of the 19th.C. Shipbuilding was initially carried out in partnership with another celebrated family, the Wigrams. The latter were also ship owners in the trade to India. Likewise, Greens owned some of these fine East Indian sailing vessels, which they operated on behalf of the East India Company or, which were engaged in their own trade to India and the Far East. The latter evolved into R & H Green's Blackwall Line of Packets to both Calcutta and, later, to Australia.

Jug used on board the Blackwall Line of Packets – manufacturer unknown.

In 1843 the Greens and Wigrams decided to dissolve their partnership and Money Wigram was one of the first of the London ship owners to transfer ships from the Indian to the Australian trade. This mainly consisted of sailings to the port of Melbourne.

Money Wigram & Sons 1864 sailing notice for their "Line of Steam &Packet ships to Australia"
(Note the similarity of the Blackwall Line and Money Wigram house flags).

BRITISH ANTARCTIC EXPEDITION

On the 26th. November 1910 Captain Robert Falcon Scott R. N. sailed from Lyttelton, New Zealand on board the whaler, TERRA NOVA, bound for the Antarctic on what proved to be a fateful expedition. The TERRA NOVA (1884/764 grt) was built at Dundee, Scotland. She had a length of 187 feet, beam of 31.4 feet and was registered at St. John's, Newfoundland and had previously been used as a relief vessel for Scott's Antarctic expedition in 1904.

Soup plate made by Dunn Bennett &Co. (apparently the manufacturers donated the china to the Expedition, as a form of publicity).

Crest of the Expedition showing the name of the vessel TERRA NOVA.
(The letters "R. Y. S." stand for the Royal Yacht Squadron. It is reported that Captain Scott joined the Royal Yacht Squadron at his own expense, so that the vessel could fly the White Ensign).

Captain Scott and four other members of his party finally reached the South Pole after great adversity in January 1912, only to find that the Norwegian explorer, Roald Amundsen, had arrived there before them. On the return journey to the TERRA NOVA the party experienced appalling weather and blizzards, finally ran out of food and all five perished.

DEVITT & MOORE

One of the most illustrious names of sailing ship owners was the firm of Devitt & Moore, whose two partners started as ship brokers on a commission basis, in the Australian trade in 1836. The first "Clipper" to be owned by them was the VIMIERA (1851/967 grt) and ,during their 55 year history, the firm owned a total of 29 square-rigged sailing ships and two steamships. This included many famous vessels, such as one of the finest passenger carrying sailing ships, the SOBRAON. She was the largest composite ship ever built (1866/2,130 grt). The first ship to be built for the company was the CITY OF ADELAIDE (1864/791 grt). She had a composite hull, with iron frames and teak hull sheathed with copper, and was used on the passenger and cargo trade, from London to Adelaide.

China mug for the "Australian Line of Steam & Clipper Ships" circa 1870 (Wm .Fairbairns).

The first of the only two steamships owned by the company was the QUEEN OF THE THAMES (1870) which was wrecked off Cape Agulhas on the coast of South Africa in March 1871, the other being the GLENELG ex. FLORENCIA (1873/1,316grt), which they owned between 1875 and 1880. However, Devitt & Moore (particularly the latter) never really took to steamships and concentrated their efforts on owning and operating their fleet of clipper ships.

In 1890 the firm started an Ocean Training Scheme which was devised by Lord Brassey and Sir Thomas Lane Devitt to train "midshipmen" as officers for the Mercantile Marine - the training ships being owned by Devitt & Moore. The venture started with two full-rigged ships, the HARBINGER and HESPERUS which were bought specially from the Orient Line for the purpose. In 1906 Devitt & Moore bought the PORT JACKSON, a beautiful four-masted barque (1882,2,212 grt), with the idea of giving square-rigged sea training to boys from the ARETHUSA, the scheme operating jointly with the Marine Society. A new company to train cadets was formed in 1909, Devitt & Moore's Ocean Training Ships Ltd., and the PORT JACKSON was joined in 1910 by a second training ship, the MEDWAY ex AMA BEGONAKOA (1902/2,516 grt). This was the final vessel of a once mighty fleet and she was sold, due to the exigencies of the First World War, to the Anglo-Saxon Petroleum Company in 1918.

This was not quite the end of the Devitt & Moore story, as in 1917 Devitt & Moore's Ocean Training Ships Ltd., purchased land at Pangbourne in Berkshire where a Nautical school to give pre-sea training was founded. In 1931 the company name was reconstructed as The Devitt & Moore Nautical College Ltd., the "Pangbourne Nautical College" ranking as highly as the two other famous nautical training colleges, H. M. S. CONWAY and H. M. S. WORCESTER, where many Merchant Navy (and Royal Navy) officers started their careers.

GREAT SHIP COMPANY

Without doubt, the GREAT EASTERN was one of the most famous and in some ways the most unsuccessful of vessels built in the middle part of the 19th.Century. Her designer was the celebrated Victorian engineer, Isambard K. Brunel and her name was initially to have been the LEVIATHAN.

Her size was impressive, 692 feet long with a beam of 120 feet across the paddle boxes and a displacement of 22,500 tons. She was laid down at the Millwall yard of Mr. John Scott Russell, a naval architect, on the 1st.May 1854 for the Eastern Steam Navigation Company. This company was incorporated by Royal Charter, and it was intended that she should carry some 4,000 passengers (800 1st.Class, 2000 2nd.Class and 1,200 3rd.Class) or 10,000 troops, in the trade to India and Australia.

A first attempt to launch her was made on 3rd. November 1857, the vessel being christened by a Miss. Hope (later the Duchess of Newcastle) before a large crowd. After the ship had moved a few feet she stuck on the launching way and there she remained, until she was finally afloat on the 31st.January 1858. Further attempts had been made to launch her in the intervening period.

Because of all the delays and costs that had been incurred, the shareholders of the Eastern Steam Navigation Company had spent £600,000 and lost a considerable sum of money. The company became defunct as a result. The Great Ship Company Limited was therefore founded by Brunel and some of the original directors, to continue with the completion of the GREAT EASTERN, as she was now named. The Great Ship Company obtained the vessel for £160,000.

Following trials, the GREAT EASTERN made her first commercial voyage in 1860, not to India and Australia for which purpose she had been designed, but to New York and with only thirty-six passengers. This was the first of a number of transatlantic voyages to America over the next few years, including at least one carrying troops, however commercially the GREAT EASTERN was a failure and the losses on her voyages led to the liquidation of the Great Ship Company Limited in 1864.

China for the GREAT EASTERN, when owned by the Great Ship Company Limited, was manufactured in Worcester by W. H. Kerr & Co. circa 1852-1862 and the pieces were top marked in the centre with a portrait of the vessel and Britannia seated alongside an anchor, in brown or light blue. On the underside the china was marked with the name of the manufacturer and some pieces (but not all) embossed with the name "Great Ship Company Limited". Decoration around the rim consisted of an anchor chain or gilt decoration, interspersed with light blue/turquoise bands.

Centre crest in brown and an example of a dinner plate

Soup plate in the blue version and W. H. Kerr's marks on the underside of the china.
(NB the embossed name "Great Ship Company Limited").

A stunning dinner plate decorated at the rim in gilt and light blue/turquoise and
detail of decoration at the rim.

As a passenger liner the GREAT EASTERN was a notable failure and never sailed to India or Australia, the purpose for which she had been envisaged. Her fate changed in 1865 when she was chartered to the electricians Glass, Elliot (who had merged in 1864 with the Gutta Percha Company to form the Telegraph Construction and Maintenance Company) - for the purpose of laying a submarine cable across the Atlantic between Great Britain and America. The vessel was modified for this task and whilst the first attempt to lay the cable was unsuccessful a second attempt in 1866 succeeded. The Telegraph Construction and Maintenance Company chartered the vessel to lay a second transatlantic cable in 1869 and she laid two further Atlantic cables for them in 1874, preceded by a cable between Bombay and Aden in 1873.

Large Telegraph Construction and Maintenance Company bowl and details of the company house flag.

Soup plate for the Telegraph Construction and Maintenance Company
(manufacturer – unknown).

Upon completion of her cable laying duties the GREAT EASTERN was laid up at Milford Haven in 1875, for the best part of twelve years. Various attempts to find work for her, including a proposal that she should be utilized as a coal hulk at Gibraltar, came to nothing.

In 1886 Messrs. Lewis and Company, who owned a number of clothiers and drapers stores in the Midlands & North of England, chartered the vessel from the then owners, London Traders Limited. Lewis & Company exhibited her and used her for popular entertainment at Liverpool. Subsequently the vessel was also exhibited at Dublin and in the river Clyde, prior to being sold by auction to metal dealers Henry Bath & Sons, who in 1888 broke the ship up at Briton Ferry, on the Mersey.

HONOURABLE EAST INDIA COMPANY
(United Company of Merchants of England trading to the East Indies)

The East India Company was incorporated on the 31st.December 1600. when it was granted a Royal Charter by Queen Elizabeth I. Apart from operating ships the company became a giant organization, with extensive trade to India and China. It eventually "ruled" India, had its own army and navy (the Bombay Marine, which was renamed the Indian Navy in 1830). It also minted its own currency.

The monopoly of the "John Company" of all trade east of the Cape of Good Hope was challenged, when a rival company, the "New" East India Company, was granted a charter in 1694. Circa 1708 the two companies amalgamated to become the "United Company of Merchants of England trading to the East Indies".

Crest of the United Company of Merchants of England trading to the East Indies and a dinner plate from the East Indiaman, LONDON of 1817(a ship of 1332.29/94 builders measurement). Spode Felspar Porcelain.

Spode Felspar Porcelain bottom mark and Chinese "chop" mark.

The first "company" ship sailed for India in 1601 and the company's vessels were armed and run on Naval lines, the Captain being known as a Commander. He was invariably a man of great professional prestige. The standard of vessels owned or chartered by the company was of the highest, with most being purpose built as stipulated by the company and to their specifications. Vessels chartered were usually owned by "gentlemen " of standing in the community and large fortunes could be made by both owners and the Commanders and senior officers of the vessels. These gentlemen were allowed cargo space for their own "private trade". The commanders also made considerable sums of money from the carriage of passengers and in their victualling.

Many of the vessels were built on the River Thames at Blackwall or Deptford and later in India, initially by shipbuilding yards in Bombay & Surat and from 1780 by shipyards in Calcutta & Chittagong. From 1786 tenders for the building of East Indiamen were thrown open to all shipbuilding yards and the Company vessels were the largest ships afloat at that time, employing very large crews which exceeded the normal manning scales, of the "ordinary" merchant vessels of the period.

China entrée dish decorated with the company crest and a dinner plate of Chinese manufacture, top marked with the "John Company" crest.

Dinner plate with an Oriental design, Alcock's Indian Iron Stone.

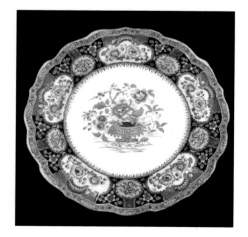

Further examples of Oriental patterns, Indian Iron Stone.

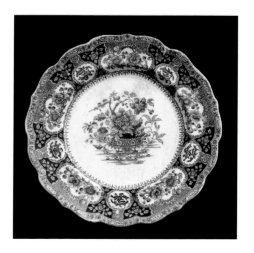

More examples of hand painted Indian Ironstone plates by John & George Alcock, circa 1839 and the Honourable East India Company back mark.

N.B. With the exception of the plate from the LONDON, there is no evidence that the pieces illustrated above were used on board East India vessels and, whilst they might have been, it is also possible that they were used in company messes in the Far East. The plates were manufactured by John & George Alcock, Corbridge, Staffordshire Potteries circa 1839-1846.

In 1813 the Company's monopoly of trade to India was terminated, the monopoly of trade to China being similarly abolished in 1833 and all the company's mercantile operations were closed by Parliament in 1834. However, the Company still continued to act as the "Government" of India until 1858. The last full meeting of the Court of Directors was held at East India House, Leadenhall Street, London on the 1st.September 1858 and the Charter of the Company, which had been renewed in 1854, finally expired in 1874.

Thus ended one of the greatest trading companies that the world has ever known

"EARL OF BALCARRES"—EAST INDIAMAN.

The EARL OF BALCARRES was a typical East Indiaman. She was built in 1811at the Bombay Dockyard, for the East India Company and was of 1417.82 builders measurement tons.

MARINE SERVICE

The plates illustrated below are somewhat of a puzzle in that, whilst there is no doubt that they were used on board various vessels, no information is to hand regarding the name of the ships or shipping companies involved, or where the plates were used.

Small bowl manufactured by Davenport, circa mid part of the 19thC.

A plate identical to the above, but decorated in dark blue, was recovered from an unknown wreck off the Welsh Coast.

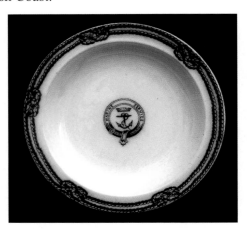  

Felspar opaque china soup plate manufactured by James Edward & Sons, Dale Hall, Burslem, Staffordshire Potteries, circa 1852. The Victorian Registration marks show that the design was first registered on the 24th.March 1852. R. Livingston, Liverpool was the supplier of the china.

An identical soup plate was recovered from the seabed at Port Phillip Bay, Melbourne, Australia confirming that china of this type was used on board vessels trading to Australia.

The anchor & crown device was also used by another shipping company trading to Australia, but with the name "Marine Service" being replaced by the name of the company i. e. Liverpool Eagle Line of Packets. This company was managed by Gibbs, Bright & Company, who started a steamship line to Australia in 1852 with the title Liverpool & Australian Navigation Company. They also operated such notable vessels as the GREAT BRITAIN and ROYAL CHARTER. Identical rope decoration around the rim was used on china used on board the GREAT BRITAIN.

Soup plate manufactured for the vessel HIOGO.

Another variation of the crown and anchor device occurs when the garter surround shows neither the name "Marine Service" or a company name, but the name of a vessel. An example is the plate from the vessel HIOGO, illustrated above.

A painting of the S. S. HIOGO by John Scott

This vessel was built in 1865 as a sailing vessel, with auxiliary steam power. She was owned by James Laing & Co, Sunderland, who were also her builders. She was wrecked circa 1870.

S. S. GREAT BRITAIN
(GREAT WESTERN STEAMSHIP COMPANY)

The GREAT BRITAIN was a screw steamer and the second of three vessels designed by the celebrated Victorian engineer, Isambard Kingdom Brunel., and the first built of iron. She was built by Patterson at Bristol for the Great Western Steamship Company in 1845 and had a displacement tonnage of 3,675 and an overall length of 322 feet.

Initially she was employed on the North Atlantic service to New York, her maiden voyage commencing on the 24th.July 1845. She later ran aground on the Northern Ireland coast at Dundrum Bay, near Belfast, on the evening of the 22nd.September 1846.

Ironstone Soup bowl

Re- floating her proved to be somewhat difficult and she was not finally afloat until August 1847, the Great Western Steamship Company having insufficient funds to carry out the necessary repairs.

In 1850 she was sold to Gibbs, Bright & Co. who extensively refitted her at Liverpool and from 1852 until 1876 she was employed on the trade between the United Kingdom & Australia, carrying emigrants. During this successful period of her career, she completed 32 round voyages to Australia (not including trooping voyages during the Crimean War).

She was then laid up at Birkenhead, for five years, before being taken over by Antony Gibbs & Sons, who employed her as a sailing vessel (without a funnel) on voyages to San Francisco. On her third voyage she experienced heavy weather near Cape Horn, and eventually put into Stanley Harbour in the Falkland Islands in a damaged condition on 24th.May 1886. Repairs were not viable and she was sold to the Falkland Islands Company for use as a floating wool warehouse.

Over the ensuing years the condition of the vessel deteriorated and in April 1937 she was beached in a leaking condition at Sparrow Point. In the 1960's much consideration was given to preserving the vessel and bringing her back to the port, where she had been built. Finally in 1968 the S.S Great Britain Project was formed and after much effort and fund raising the GREAT BRITAIN was loaded on a pontoon on the 11th. April 1970, for the voyage to the United Kingdom.

The pontoon was towed to Bristol by the tug VARIUS II and after a lengthy tow the GREAT BRITAIN arrived at Avonmouth on the 24th.June 1970. The decision was eventually taken to keep the vessel at Bristol and she was placed in the Great Western Dock, where she had originally been built. Since then considerable restoration has been carried out and the vessel has become a very popular prize winning tourist attraction.

Crest of the china – note the word "Saloon". Suppliers of the china to the GREAT BRITAIN were J. Stonier & Company, Liverpool.

Copy of a contemporary sailing notice, when the GREAT BRITAIN was sailing between England & Australia.

Sources of Information and selected Bibliography

Encyclopaedia of British Pottery & Porcelain Marks – Geoffrey A. Godden

Houseflags

Lloyd's List of House Flags published in 1882

Lloyd's Book of House Flag & Funnels published in 1904 and 1912

Flags National & Mercantile House Flags & Funnels by Griffin & Company, Portsmouth

"S. S. House Flags" and "Reed's Flags and Funnels" by Thomas Reed & Co. Ltd, Sunderland

Brown's Flags & Funnels (nine editions) by Brown, Son & Ferguson, Ltd., Glasgow Flags, Funnels and Hull Colours" published by Adlard Coles Limited.

Charts depicting House Flags & Funnels published by the Liverpool Journal of Commerce

House-Flags and Funnels of British and Foreign Shipping Companies" drawn and edited by E. C Talbot-Booth in 1937

A Survey of Mercantile Houseflags & Funnels" by J. L. Loughran, published by Waine Research Publications in 1979

General

A Celebration of the Sea by Rina Prentice published by the National Maritime Museum, Greenwich

Encyclopaedia of Ships & Shipping edited by Herbert B Mason

The Cube Teapot – Anne Anderson published by Richard Dennis 1999

Merchant Fleets in Profile by Duncan Haws

Merchant Fleets by Duncan Haws

Merchant Ships of the World in Colour 1910-1929 Laurence Dunn

North Atlantic Seaway by N R P Bonsor (five volumes)

South Atlantic Seaway by N R P Bonsor

A Century of North Sea Passenger Steamers by Ambrose Greenway

Great Passenger Ships of the World (six volumes) by Arnold Kludas

Travels of the Tramps (five volumes) by Norman L Middlemiss

Records by Ships in Focus Publications, Preston

British Shipping Fleets by Roy Fenton and John Clarkson – Ships in Focus Publications

Passenger Ships of Australia & New Zealand (two volumes), Peter Plowman

British Passenger Liners of the Five Oceans by Commander C R Vernon Gibbs

British Ocean Tramps – Volume 2. Owners & Their Ships by P N Thomas

North Star to Southern Cross by John M Maber

Across the Irish Sea Belfast - Liverpool Shipping Since 1819 by Robert C Sinclair

Cableships and Submarine Cables by K R Haigh

West Coast Steamers – Duckworth & Langmuir

Periodicals & magazines

Ships Monthly Magazine, Burton on Trent

Sea Breezes Magazine, Douglas, Isle of Man

Shipping Today and Yesterday Magazine, St. Leonards on Sea

Shipping Company histories

Aberdeen Line – The Sea Carriers 1825-1925 by L Cope Cornford

Anchor Line 1856-1956 by R S McLellan

Ravenscraig – The Allan Royal Mail Line by Thomas E Appleton

Asiatic Steam Navigation Co. Ltd 1878-1963 by W A Laxon (W.S.S.)

The Australian Commonwealth Shipping Line by Frank Brennan

Atlantic Royal Mail Steam Navigation Company – The Galway Line - Transatlantic Triumph & Heroic Failure by Timothy Collins

Bailey and Leetham by Arthur Credland and Richard Greenwood – Ships in Focus

Bank Line – Seventy Adventurous Years 1885-1955 Journal of Commerce, Liverpool

The Ben Line – The History of a Merchant Fleet 1825 – 1955 by George Blake

The Ben Line 1825-1982 An Anecdotal History by Michael Strachan

Blue Funnel – A history of Alfred Holt & Company 1865-1914 by Francis E Hyde

The Blue Funnel Legend – A History of the Ocean Steam Ship Company 1865-1973 by Malcolm Falkus

Blue Star Line 1939-1945 by Taffrail

Blue Star by Tony Atkinson and Kevin O'Donoghue (W.S.S.)

The Bowring Story by David Keir

Benjamin Bowring and His Descendants by Arthur C Wardle

Booth Line by P.M.Heaton

A Liverpool Merchant House Being the History of Alfred Booth & Company 1863-1958 by A H John

B.I Centenary 1856-1956 – The Story of the British India Steam Navigation Co. Ltd by George Blake

Sea Safari – British India S N Co. African Ships & Services by Peter C Kohler

B I – The British India Steam Navigation Company Limited by W A Laxon & F W Perry (W.S.S.)

The History of the Bibby Line by E W Paget-Tomlinson

The Bibby Line 1807-1990 A Story of Wars, Booms & Slumps by Nigel Watson

Brocklebanks 1770-1950 (two volumes) by John Frederic Gibson

The Lady Boats – The Life & Times of Canada's West Indies Merchant Fleet by Felicity Hanington

Canadian Pacific – The Story of the Famous Shipping Line by George Musk

History of the Canadian Pacific Line by Frank C Bowen

The China Navigation Company Limited - A pictorial History 1872-1992 , published by Butterfield & Swire/John Swire & Sons

The Clan Line in the Great War by Archibald Heard

Gathering of the Clans – History of The Clan Line Steamers Ltd by N L Middlemiss

A Victorian Shipowner by Augustus Muir and Mair Davies (Clan Line)

Cunard and the North Atlantic 1840-1973 by Francis E Hyde

The Cunard Story by Howard Johnson

Cunard White Star Liners of the 1930's by Richard P De Kerbrech & David L Williams

Painted Ports – The story of the ships of Messrs Devitt and Moore by Captain A G Course

The Donaldson Line – A Century of Shipping 1854-1954 by Alastair M Dunnett

Donaldson Line by P J Telford

DP & L A History of the Dundee, Perth & London Shipping Company Ltd and Associated Shipping Companies by Graeme Somner (W.S.S.)

The East India Company and its Ships by Jean Sutton

The East India Company by Antony Wild

The Trade Makers – Elder Dempster in West Africa 1852-1972 by P N Davies

The Conquest of the Niger by Land and Sea by David Hollett (Elder Dempster)

Elder Dempster Fleet History 1852-1985 by James E Cowden & John O C Duffy

Ellermans - A Wealth of Shipping by James Taylor

Ellermans in South Africa 1892-1992 by Kenneth Payne & Ulick Brown

Furness Withy 1891-1991 by David Burrell (W.S.S.)

Furness-Houlder Lines by Norman L Middlemiss

Fyffes and the Banana – A Centenary History 188-1988 by Peter N Davies

Yes! We Have Some – The Story of Fyffes by Patrcick Beaver

Semper Fidelis – The Saga of the "Navvies" 1924-1948 by H E Hancock (G.S.N.C.)

'The Navvies' – History of the General Steam Navigation Company by Norman L Middlemiss

A Century of Sea Trading by L Cope Cornford (G.S.N.C.)

Glen Line to the Orient by E P Harnack

The Great Iron Ship by James Dugan (S.S.GREAT EASTERN)

Shipping Enterprise and Management 1830-1939 Harrisons of Liverpool by Francis E Hyde

Over a Century and a Quarter of Progress – The Charente Steam-Ship Co.Ltd.

Paddy Henderson – The Story of P Henderson & Company by Dorothy Laird

Irrawaddy Flotilla by Alister McCrae & Alan Prentice

One Hundred Years of Houlders by Edward F Stevens

H Hogarth & Sons Ltd - The Baron Line by Gray (W.S.S.)

Huntings of Newcastle upon Tyne – Company

Island Lifeline by Connery Chappell (Isle of Man SP Co.)

Lamport & Holt by P M Heaton

History of Lyle Shipping Company Limited by Michael Crowdy (W.S.S.)

From Cape to Cape – The History of Lyle Shipping by John Orbell

The Saga of Manchester Liners by Robert B Stoker

60 Years on the Western Ocean by R B Stoker (Manchester Liners)

In the Wake of Endeavour – The History of the New Zealand Shipping Company and Federal Steam Navigation Company by Gordon Holman

Clipper Ship to Motor Liner - The story of the New Zealand Shipping Company 1873-1939 by Sydney D Waters

Crossed Flags – The Histories of the New Zealand Shipping Company – Federal Steam Navigation Company and their subsidiaries by W A Laxon, I J Farquhar, N J Kirby & F W Perry (W.S.S.)

Origins, Orient and Oriana by Charles F Morris (Orient Line)

By Royal Charter – The Steam Conquistadores – A history of the Pacific Steam Navigation Company by John E Lingwood

Steam Conquers the Pacific by Arthur C Wardle

P&O – A Hundred Year History of the Peninsular and Oriental Steam Navigation Co. 1837-1937 by Boyd Cable

The Story of P&O by David Howarth and Stephen Howarth

P&O – A Fleet History by Stephen Rabson and Kevin O'Donoghue

Port Line by H C Spong & J Dobson (W.S.S.)

Ritsons' Branch Line by Malcolm Cooper (W.S.S.)

125 Years of Maritime History 1839-1964 – Royal Mail Lines Limited

Macqueen's Legacy – Ships of the Royal Mail Line – Volumes One & Two by Stuart Nicol

A Business of National Importance – The Royal Mail Shipping Group 1902-1937 by Edwin Green and Michael Moss

Shaw Savill & Albion – The Post-War Fortunes of a Shipping Empire by Richard P de Kerbrech

Shaw Savill Line – One Hundred Years of Trading by Sydney D Waters

The Flag of the Southern Cross by Frank C Bowen

The Shire Line by W A Laxon

Union- Castle Chronicle 1853-1953 by Marischal Murray

The Cape Run by W H Mitchell and L A Sawyer

Union-Castle Line by Peter Newall

Union Line – A short history of the Union Steam Ship Company of New Zealand Limited 1875-1951 by Sydney D Waters

A Century of Style – Great Ships of the Union Line 1875-1976 by N H Brewer

Union Fleet by Ian Farquhar (Union Steam Ship Company of New Zealand)

The Wilson Line of Hull 1831-1981 by Arthur C Credland and Michael Thompson

The Wilson Line by Arthur C Credland

Wilson Line by John Harrower (W.S.S.)

The White Star Line – An Illustrated History 1869-1934 by Paul Louden-Brown

The Ismay Line by Wilton J Oldham (White Star)

White Star by Roy Anderson

Sunward by Yeowards – The First 100 Years by Barry

Libraries & Museums

Glasgow University Archives

The Library, The National Maritime Museum, Greenwich, London

Public Records Office, Kew, London

INDEX OF COMPANIES

Numbers in **BOLD** refer to the pages where an article on a specific company history, is located.

PLEASE NOTE
Pages 1 to 14 and Pages 311 to 323 are to be found in both Volume One and Volume Two
Pages 15 to Page 144 are to be found only in Volume One
Pages 145 to Page 310 are to be found only in Volume Two